CONTENTS

Why not have a go at making the birds in sizes
that will fit in your hand using some soft and fluffy wool?

Handcrafting the birds means that you'll get a different effect every time you make one, which is also part of the fun.

This book brings together a wide-ranging collection of birds, including parrots, parakeets, and many other kinds.

Enjoy making a bird that looks like your pet or as a gift to your friends.

You can try any of your favorite birds at your hand.

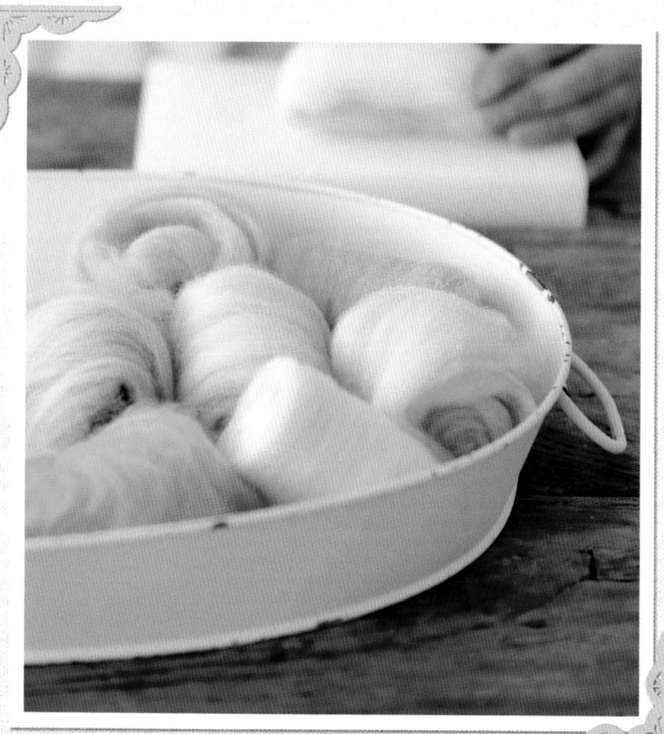

Working on wools of assorted colours, we simply jab away with a specially designed felting needle for the fibres to mesh and form into shapes.

You'll enjoy the process of gradually shaping the birds, and amazed by the finished designs!

Budgerigar

Budgerigar

Of all the parrots, the most popular is the budgerigar,with its distinctive combinations of blue, yellow, and other colours.

Did you know that blue at the top of the beak indicates the male, and pink the female?

1
2

3

How to make Page 36

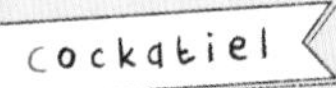
cockatiel

Cockatiel

The cockatiel is marked out by its jauntily elongated crest and orange cheeks. Those puffy cheeks are another attractive feature.

4

5

How to make Page 44

Rosy-faced Lovebird

Rosy-faced Lovebird

Good day. I'm the rosy-faced lovebird, looking as though butter wouldn't melt in my mouth. I have this habit of tilting my head to one side.

6

How to make Page 46

Galah

Galah

As its other name, the pink and grey, suggests, the galah is beautifully pink-coloured parrot. It sports a splendid tufty crest on its head. The galah is found in Australia.

How to make Page 48

Lovebird

With its unique, vivid colouring, the Lilian's lovebird seems to have a habit of snuggling straight into any narrow space that it spots.

Being a lovebird, it shows tenderness towards its partner, and so easily becomes attached to its owner too, hence its popularity.

9
8

How to make Page 49

Monk Parakeet

Monk Parakeet

The monk parakeet has a scalloped pattern on its breast. Its name seems to have come from the idea that its neck markings look like a monk's hood.

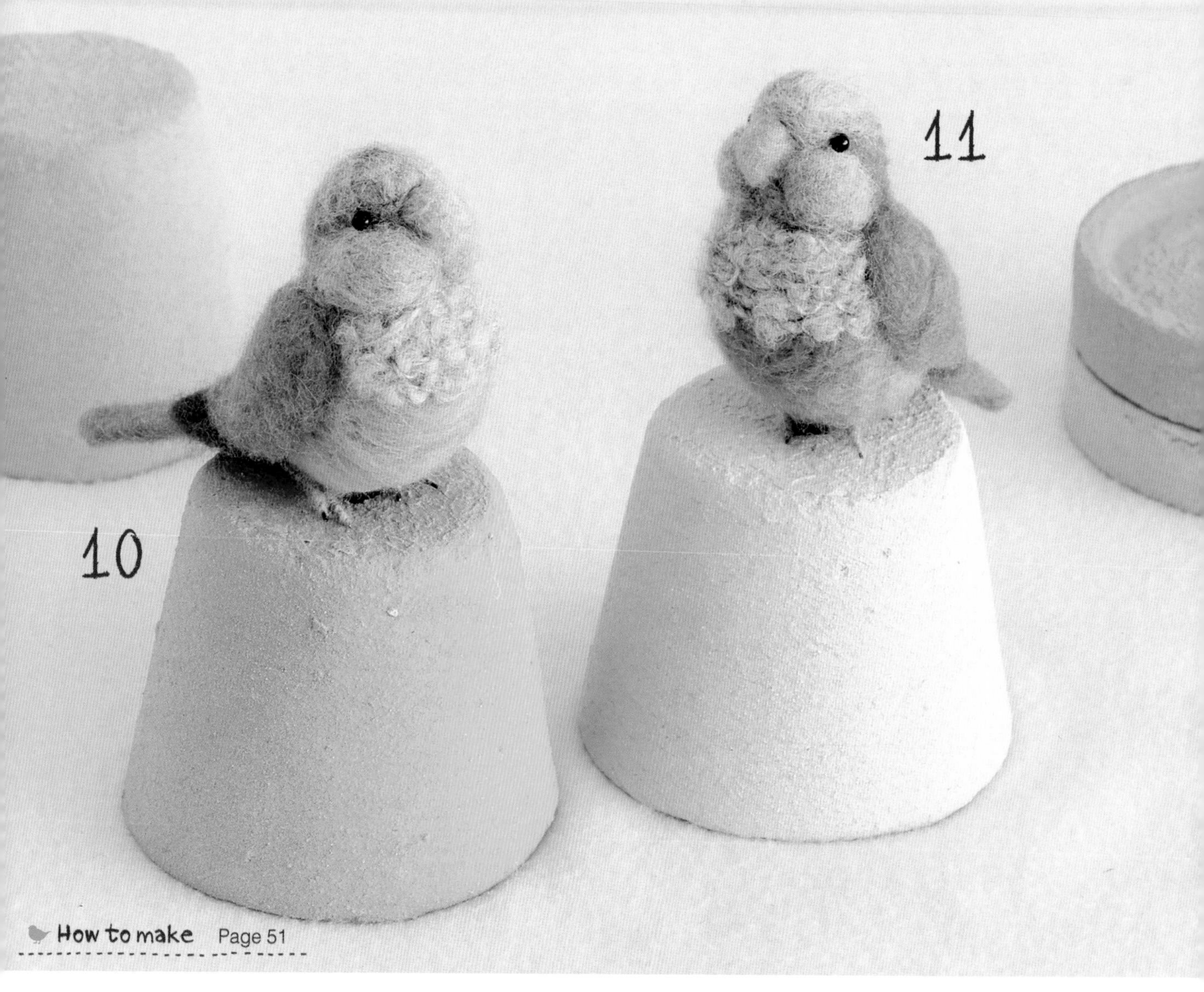

11

10

How to make Page 51

Bourke's Parrot

The Bourke's parrot is also found in various colours, of which this is the popular rubino. Its light pink body and yellow accents are so cute.

12

How to make Page 52

White-bellied Parrot

The white-bellied parrot is named for its appearance. It is also known as a delightful bird that will roll over playfully of its own accord.I've made mine posing with one leg lifted up.

13

How to make Page 53

Eastern Rosella

The eastern rosella is distinguished by its vivid red, blue, and yellow colouring. The scale pattern on its back and wings is another trademark. Being able to make complex patterns simply is one of the features of wool felt.

14

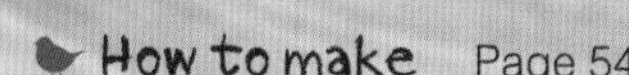

How to make Page 54

Scarlet Macaw

The macaw is the largest of the parrot gang. Although under natural conditions some reach close to a metre in length, I've made them in a dinky size that will fit in your hand.

15

How to make Page 56

Blue and Yellow Macaw

The kabuki-actor face patterns are comical, and the bird looks great glancing backwards like this.

16

How to make Page 58

Sulphur-crested Cockatoo

The sulphur-crested cockatoo has the gift of the gab. This parrot is distinguished by its white body and yellow crest. The bird on the right with blue markings around the eyes is the triton cockatoo.

17
18

How to make Page 60

Toco Toucan

Toco Toucan

The large orange beak is a real standout.
A fruit-loving bird from the tropics.

19

How to make Page 62

20
21

Java Sparrow

The Java sparrow is a familiar pet. Number 20 is the white variety, while the number 21 is the pied Java sparrow. The two different-coloured birds will make a lovely pair.

How to make Page 64

Japanese Wild Birds

I've tried making some of the wild birds that we're used to seeing around us in Japan in tiny sizes. You can make all three with the same base shape.

Red-flanked bluetail
22

Warbling white-eye
23

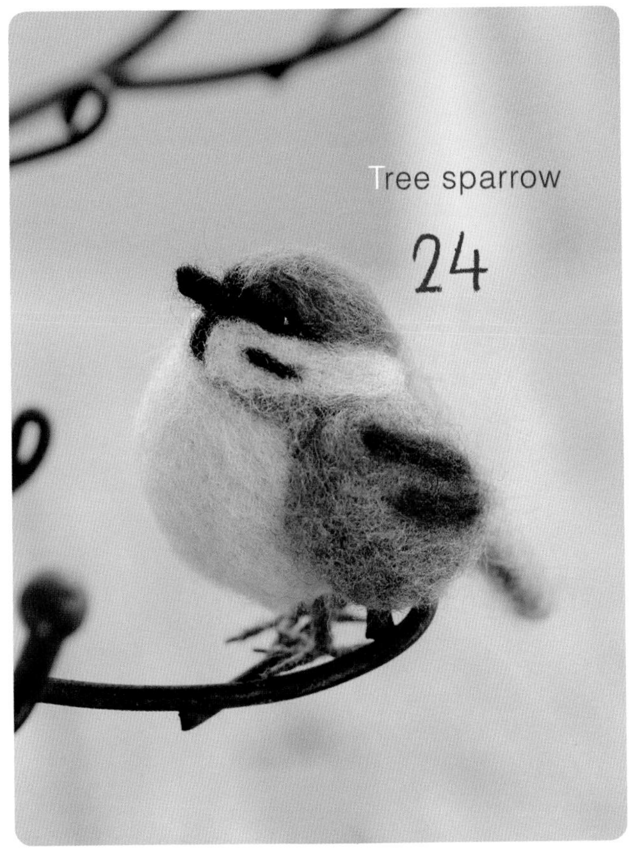
Tree sparrow
24

How to make

22 - p.66 23 - p.67

24 - p.68

Beautiful Birds in the World

The Japanese kingfisher and other birds from the rest of the world with beautiful colourings.With the Cuban tody, which is as dinky as a hummingbird, and the lilac-breasted roller, whose plumage contains 14 colours, I've tried my hand at some more unusual birds.

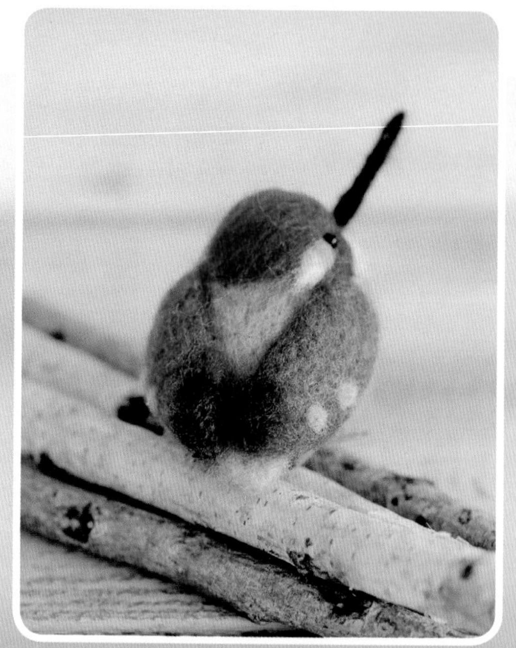

Kingfisher

25

Cuban tody

26

Lilac-breasted roller

27

How to make

25 - p.69　26 - p.70

27 - p.71

Flamingo

Flamingo

The long-legged flamingo. I make the legs by wrapping wool around a core. They look lovely on their own, but it's a nice idea to make a few to form a group.

28

How to make Page 72

Shoebill

Shoebill

29

The shoebill is currently very popular in zoos. Standing stock still, it's a bird with a mysterious aura.

How to make Page 74

30
Scarlet macaw

33
Rosy-faced lovebird

31
Budgerigar

32
Owl

34
Major Mitchell's cockatoo

Bird Brooch

Bird Brooch

I've made wool brooches in semi-3D by deconstructing some of the birds. They're easier to make than 3D designs, so I'd recommend them for beginners too.

How to make 30 - p.76 31 & 32 - p.77 33 - p.42 34 - p.78

Egg

Eggs

Simple eggs made by felting the wool into a round shape.

Make them in different colours for a fun effect. I've added the letters to make up the word SMILE.

35

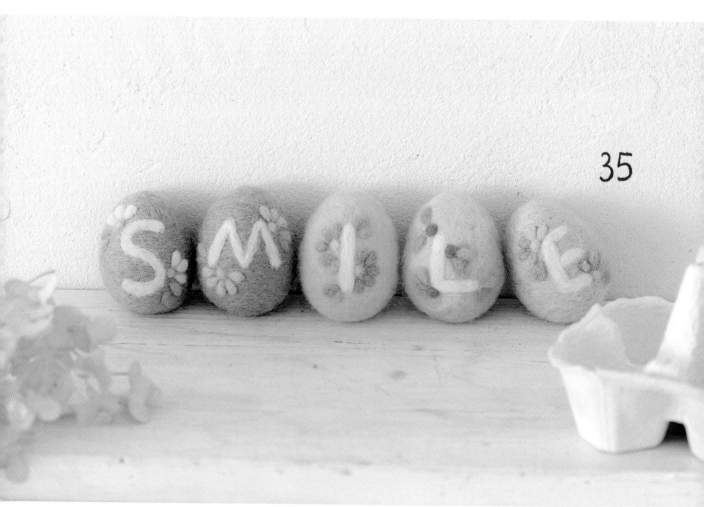

How to make Page 79

Feature

Cherry (♂ age 11)

The parrots who live in my home

Chelsea (♂ age 9)

My life felting wool with my parrots around me

We currently have in our home rosy-faced lovebird Cherry (♂ age 11) and cockatiel Chelsea (♂ age 9).

In human terms, they'd both be something like old men or granddads, I suppose. Cherry is curious about everything. The moment she comes across a new thing, she goes straight for it. Chelsea on the other hand is timid. If she doesn't know something, she pretends not to see it. Although they couldn't be more different, they get on very well with one another, and fly freely around the home together whenever it's their time to be let out.

When I'm making something, curious-about-everything Cherry will come over and take the materials in her beak or have a meddle. And yet both Cherry and Chelsea seem to not to like the imitation parrots that I make. If I try to take a two shot of them with a imitation parrot alongside a real one, they won't let me. I would like to try sneaking one into the birdcage with them, but... :-)

Face to face with a wool parrot...

Cherry is mischievous. Even when I'm making things, he'll come and meddle.

Chelsea might be timid, but he has a healthy appetite.

Like a display at an exhibition. All kinds of birds set out in a line.

I keep my wool in drawers, sorted into blues, yellows and the rest of the colours. I take pleasure in even just looking at colourful wool.

This is how my monthly lessons look. We all chatter noisily as we work away with our needles...

I've loved pets ever since I was a child, and have had all sorts of creatures, including budgerigars, Java finches, society finches, canaries, hamsters, and Pomeranians. Out of them all, I particularly love small birds, which I've tried to make using various craft techniques. Clay, beads, knitted stuffed toys... I was beginning to think I'd never get them the way I wanted when I came across some wool felt at a craft shop. I fell for the soft, fluffy feel of the material, so easy to shape in any way you like. I made all sorts of things, putting them out in my room.

While I was doing all of this, I made up my mind to show the birds that I'd made at a flea market, and went along to a local event. I set them out on an outdoor table, and lots of people came over and picked them up. They included folk who had fond memories of keeping birds in the past, and children who took them home cradled preciously in the palm of their hand... Things that I'd made could touch someone's heart. Experiencing this pleasure was the start of my wool felting days.

As well as giving my regular monthly lessons, I show my work at seasonal events and department store functions, and participate in workshops for kids as a volunteer. I love to be there at the moment when people shout an appreciative "Done it!", and have gone as far as Osaka and Hiroshima as well as Tokyo, Kanagawa, and Chiba closer to home. My current aim is to conquer all 47 prefectural areas of Japan. I would love to get lots more people into wool felt, and for them to pass on to others the joys of making things with it.

Miwa Utsunomiya

The birds also make fun presents to give your friends. Make an effort with the wrapping too.

Technique Guide

Basic materials

Wool

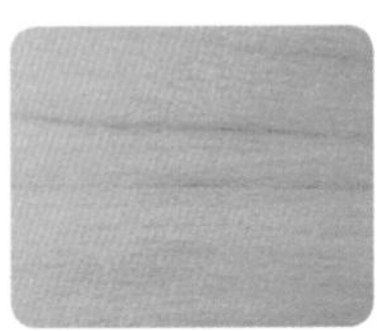

Solid

A standard type of wool suited to making a broad range of designs. Comes in a rich variety of colours.

Natural Blend
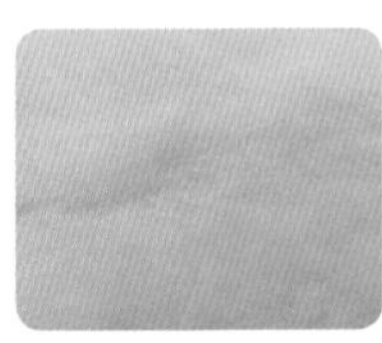

Natural Blend

Easy-to-use, natural-coloured wool. Its shortish fibres and slightly rougher texture bring out rustic nuances.

Mix
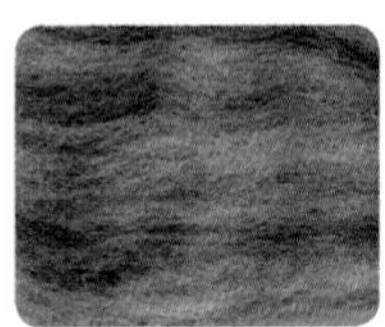

Mix

A blend of wools in the same colour tones that helps bring out depth of expression.

FELTING YARN
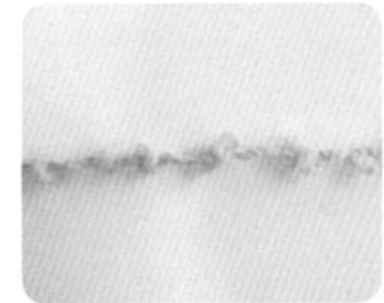

Felting yarn loop

Fluffy, curled yarn. To use it, felt it in place with a felting needle.

Needle Watawata

Needle Watawata

Fleecy wool that meshes together with only light jabbing. Ideal for making bases for your designs.

Other materials

Solid eyes

The eye components. The size to use depends on the design.

Clear plastic wallet

To use as a template when making the wings.

Tekno Rote

A material that can be bent freely and holds its shape, like wire. To use for the core when making things like tail feathers. We are using the 0.7-mm diameter variety.

Basic tools

Felting needle

Specially shaped at the ends so that the fibres mesh and form into felt when you jab into the wool. The needle on the right is extra fine.

Felting mat

A mat to lay out underneath when you are working with a felting needle.

Scissors

Craft scissors.

Finger guard

Protects your fingers from the needle.

手芸用
クラフトボンド

Craft glue

Quick-drying glue that is clear when dry. For attaching the eyes and other components.

Tailors Awl

For making holes in which to insert the eye components.

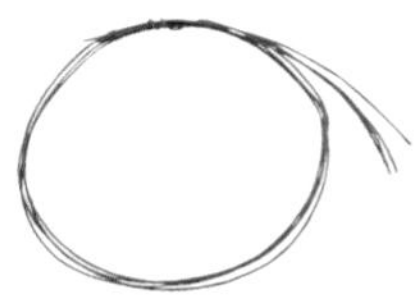

Floral wire (brown, 24 gauge)

Wire wrapped in thin, brown paper tape. For the core of the legs. Available from craft stores.

Floral tape

Tape used for things like flower arrangements. Stretch the tape by pulling gently on it as you wrap and it becomes adhesive, allowing you to wind it neatly around wire. Available from craft stores.

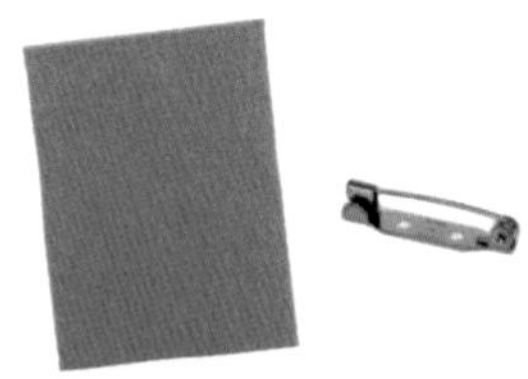

Felt and brooch pin

For making bird brooches.

How to make the bases for the birds

The birds in this book are made from the three bases shown below. In this section, we get to grips with how to make the bases.

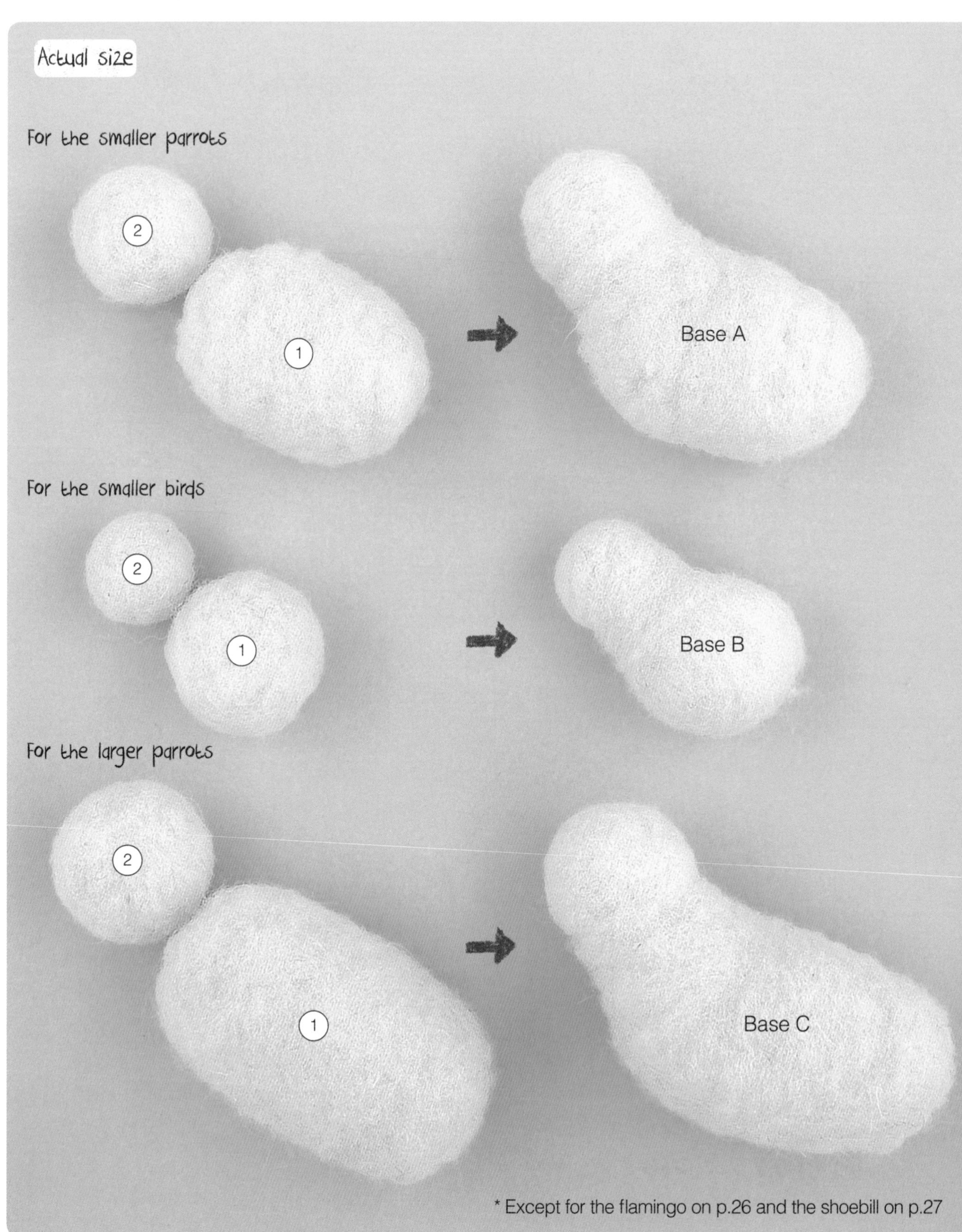

Actual size
For the smaller parrots
2
1
Base A
For the smaller birds
2
1
Base B
For the larger parrots
2
1
Base C

* Except for the flamingo on p.26 and the shoebill on p.27

1 Make the ball marked ①
Tear off some natural blend wool with your fingers, taking a suitable amount in your hand.

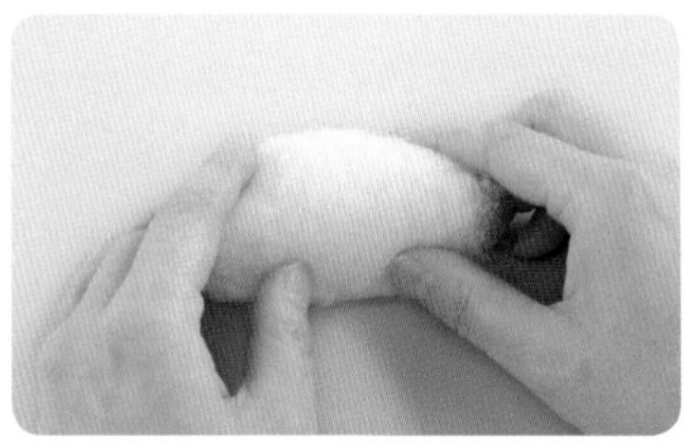

2 As a guideline, the amount you're looking for will make something like the finished size when squeezed tightly in your hand.

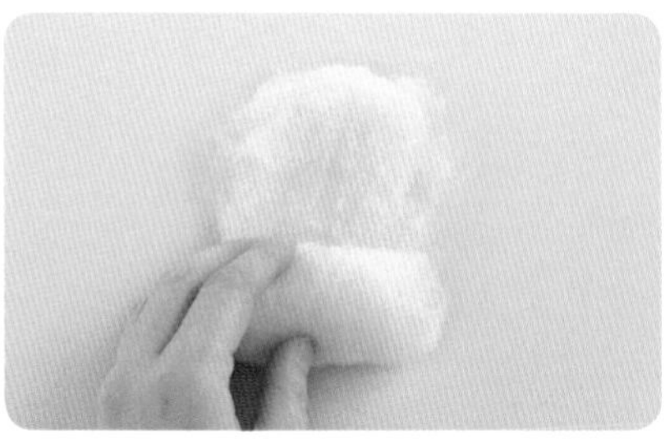

3 Roll up the strip of the wool from one end.

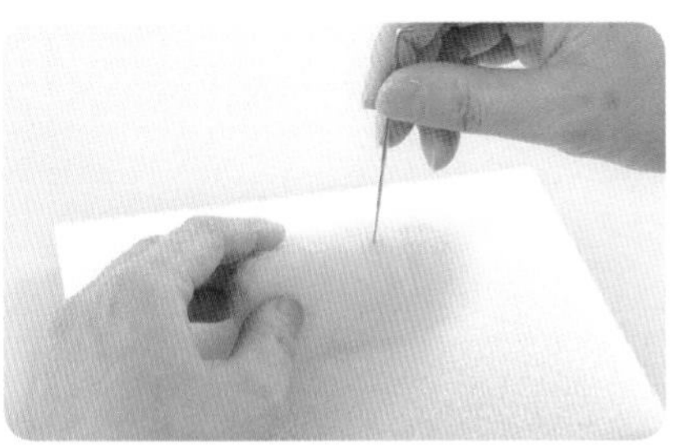

4 Place it on the mat and stab it all over with the needle.

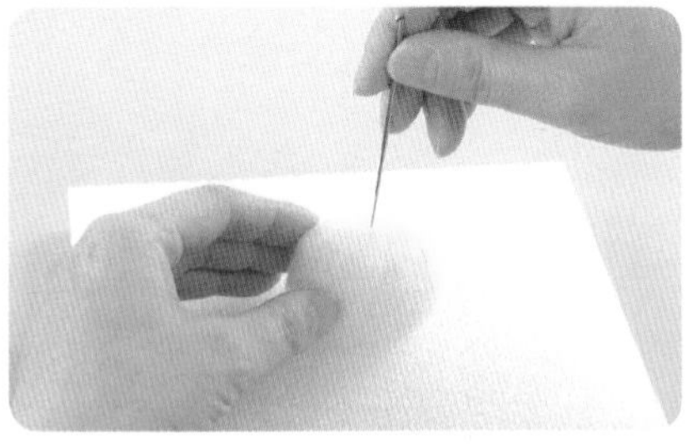

5 As you felt it, it will gradually form into the size and shape of the actual-size photograph on the left-hand page. If it's too small, add more wool and continue felting it in.

6 ① The completed ball marked.

7 Make the ball marked ②
Make the ball marked ② in the same way.

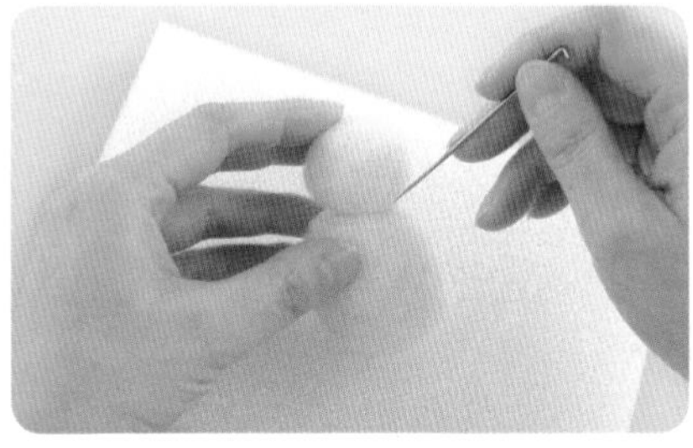

8 Join ① and ②
Put balls and ② together and felt them onto one another with the needle.

9 This is how they should look when joined together.

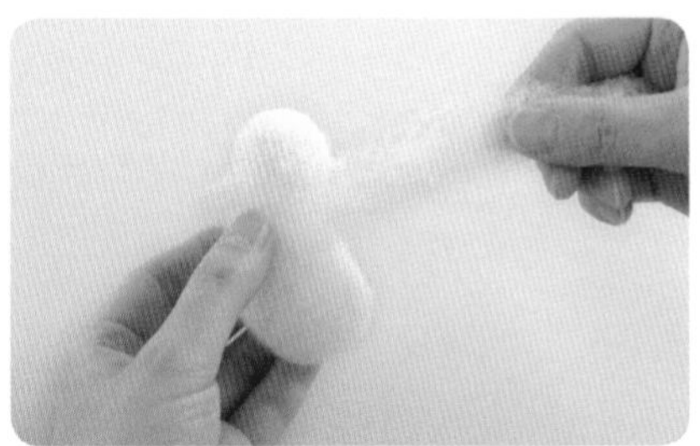

10 Flesh the shape out
Take a small amount of wool and wrap it around the join.

11 Jab it with the needle to smooth it out.

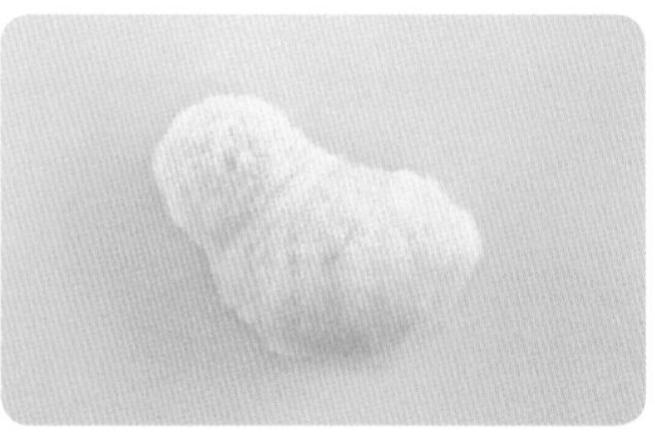

12 This is how it looks on completion.

Process Guide

In this section, I'll show you the basic procedure for making the birds.

We'll be making the budgerigar on pp.4 and 5

1
2
3

See p. 41 for the full-scale design and colour scheme

Make base A on p.34 before you start!

I'll be explaining using the bird numbered 1 in the picture above

Materials for 1

Felt wool

Solid	•Off-white, 4 g •Yellow-green, 3 g •Violet-blue •Saxe blue •Beige •Light pink, small amounts
Natural Blend	•Custard, 3 g
Mix	•Black, small amount

Materials for 2

Felt wool

Solid	•Off-white, 4 g •Aqua, 3.5 g •White, 2 g •Violet-blue •Light pink, small amounts
Natural Blend	•Grey •Custard, small amounts

Materials for 3

Felt wool

Solid	•Off-white, 4 g •Saxe blue, 3.5 g •White, 2 g •Violet-blue •Light pink, small amounts
Natural Blend	•Custard, small amount
Mix	•Navy blue, small amount

Common materials

Solid eyes
•3.5 mm x 2

Other materials

•Clear plastic wallet 2 cm × 12 cm
•Floral wire (brown, 24 gauge) 8 x 3-cm lengths
•Tekno Rote, 16 cm
•Floral tape, amount to suit

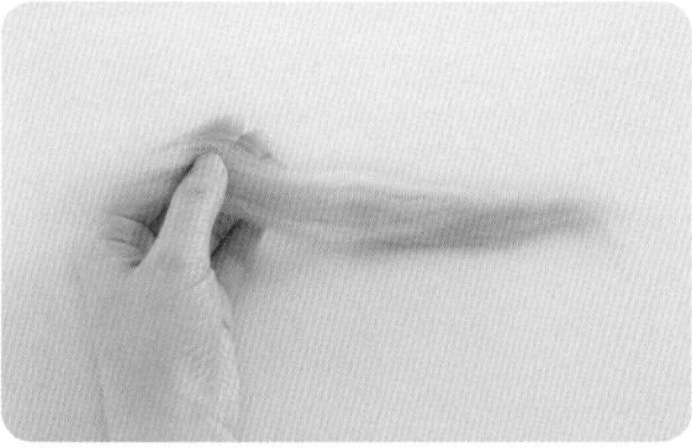

1 Add colour to the base
Tear off some yellow-green wool and take a small amount on your hand.

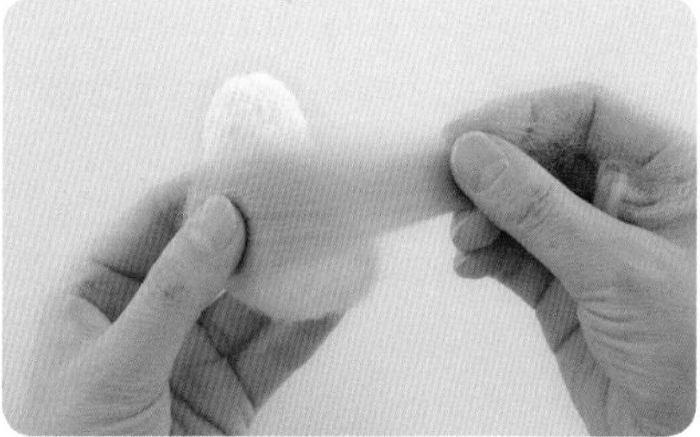

2 Wrap it onto the base.

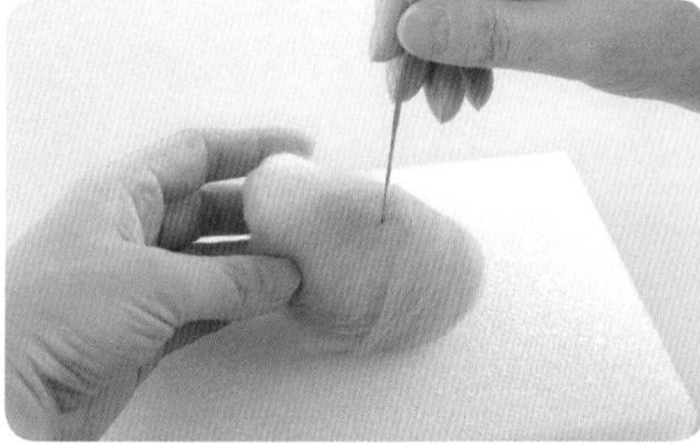

3 Jab carefully with the needle to even out the surface. Sticking the needle in too deep will make hollows in the base, so work gently and jab only the surface.

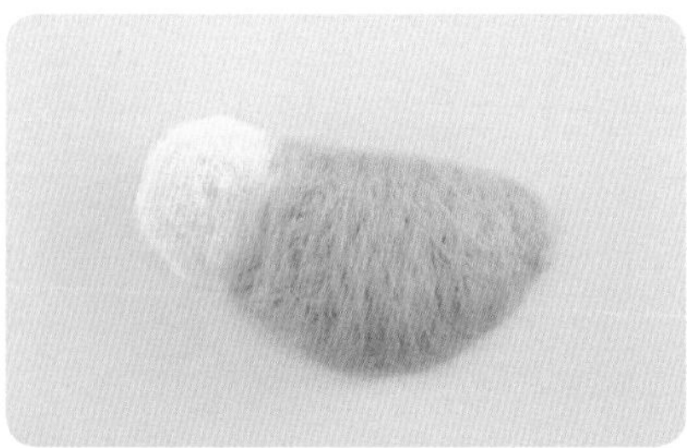

4 The body is now coloured in.

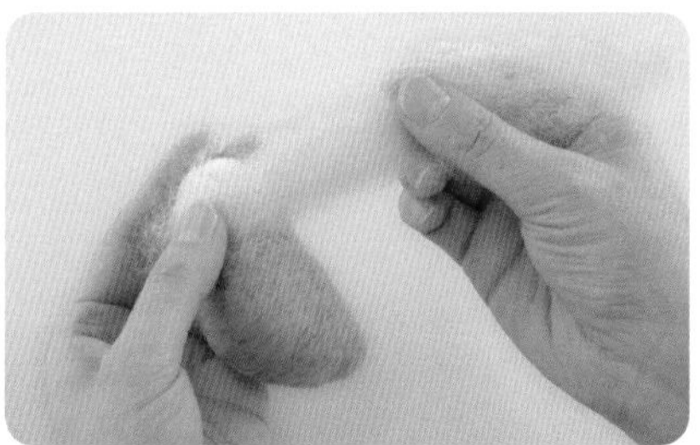

5 Wrap some custard wool around the head section.

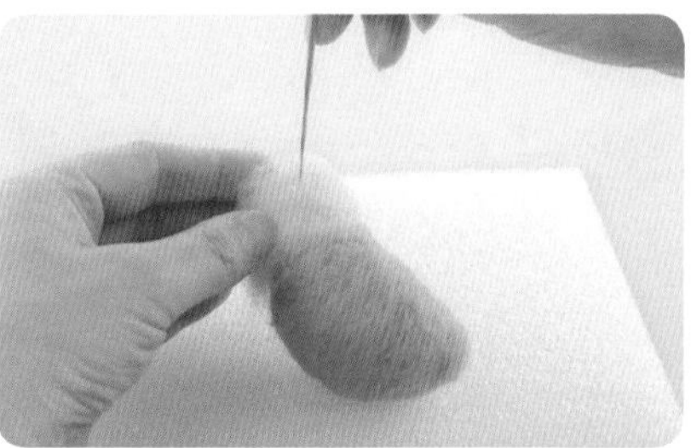

6 Jab carefully with the needle to even out the surface.

7 The face is now coloured in.

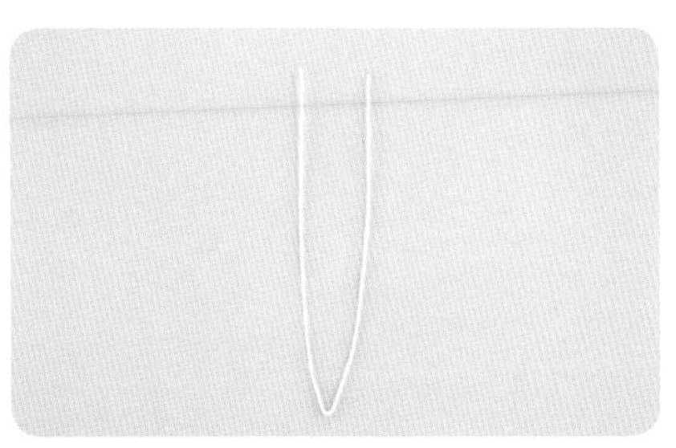

8 Make the tail feather
Bend the Tekno Rote in half as shown in the picture.

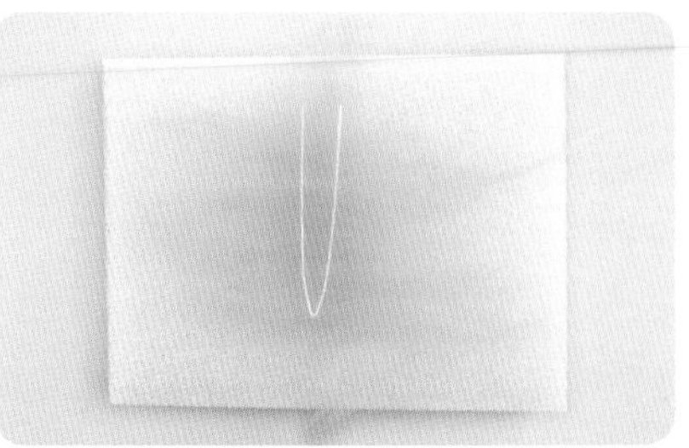

9 Loosen some wool into thin wisps and spread it out so that the fibres extend both vertically and horizontally. Place the Tekno Rote on top of the wool.

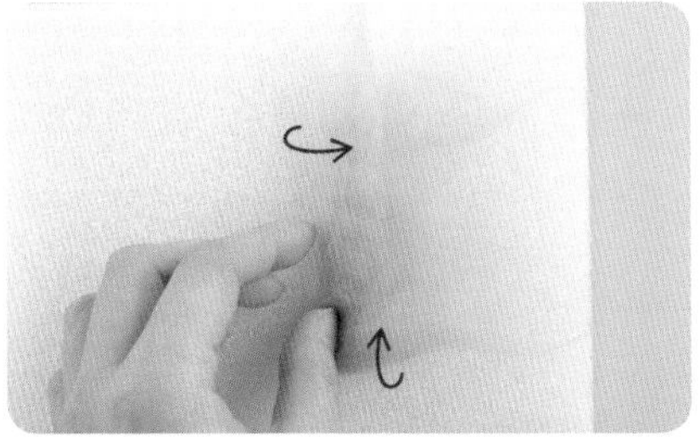

10 Fold the left-hand side and bottom of the wool so as to envelop the Tekno Rote.

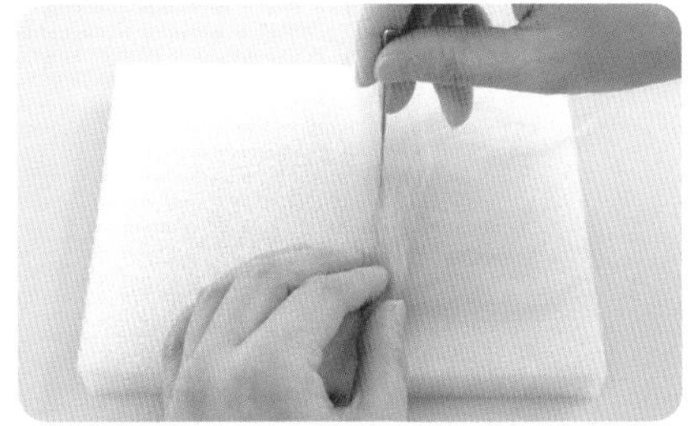

11 Felt in place with the needle.

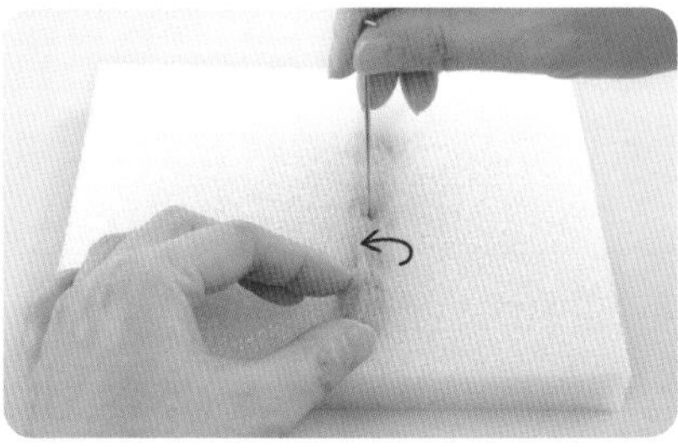

12 Now wrap the right-hand side of the wool over, jabbing with the needle to smooth it out.

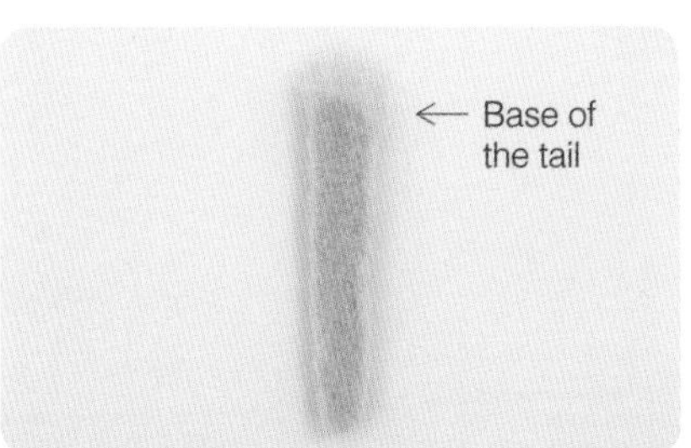
← Base of the tail

13 This is how the tail feather looks on completion. Leave the area at the base of the tail wispy.

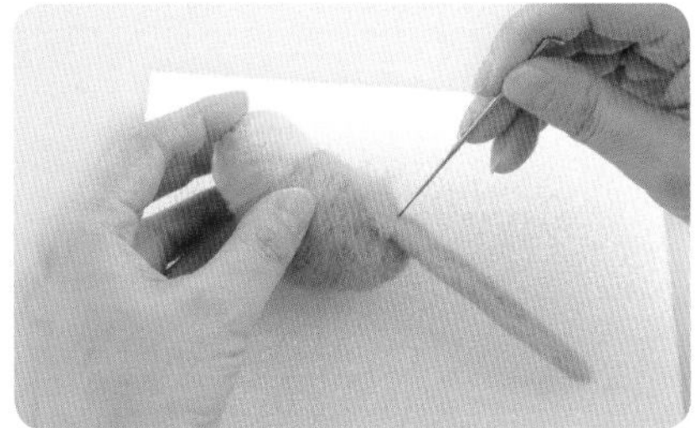

14 Attach the tail feather to the body. Felt the area that you've left wispy onto the body, securing it firmly in place.

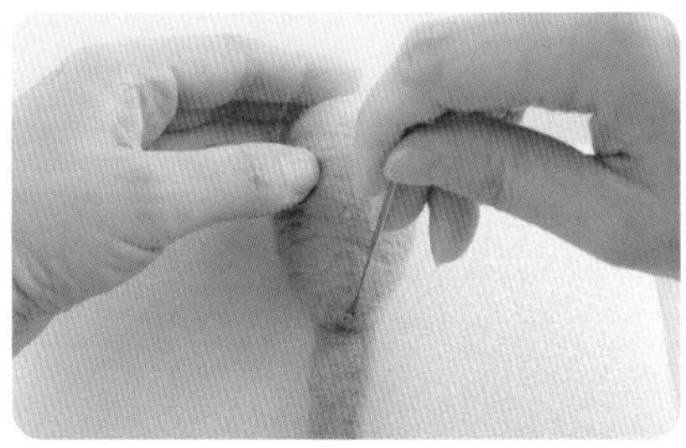

15 Felt firmly from the underside too.

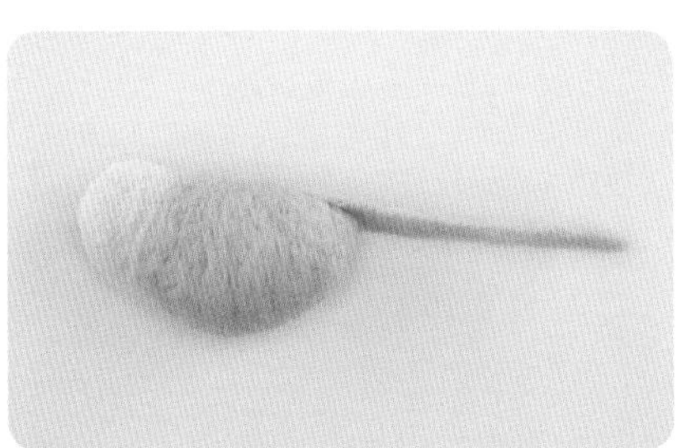

16 This is how it looks once the tail feather is attached.

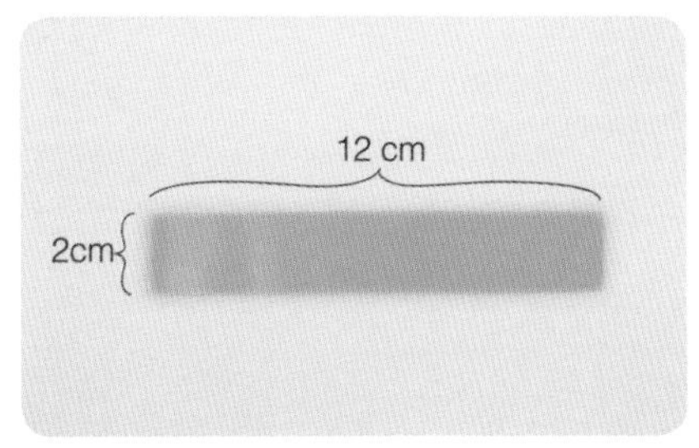
12 cm
2cm

17 Make the wings.
Cut the clear plastic wallet with a cutter.

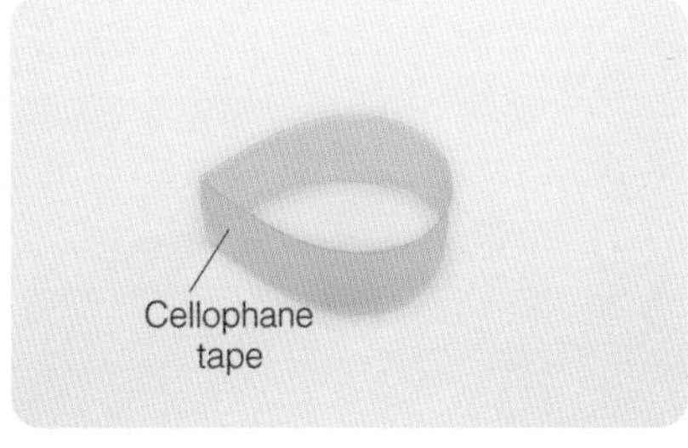
Cellophane tape

18 Curl into a droplet shape and fasten together with cellophane tape.

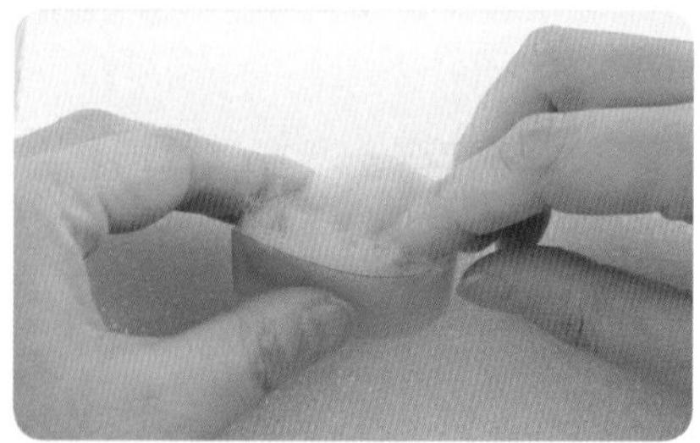

19 Pack with custard wool.

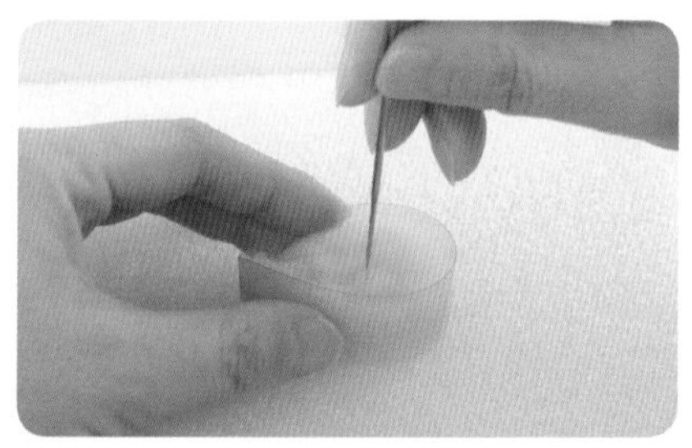

20 Felt with the needle until compact. Occasionally turn the shape over to felt it from the reverse.

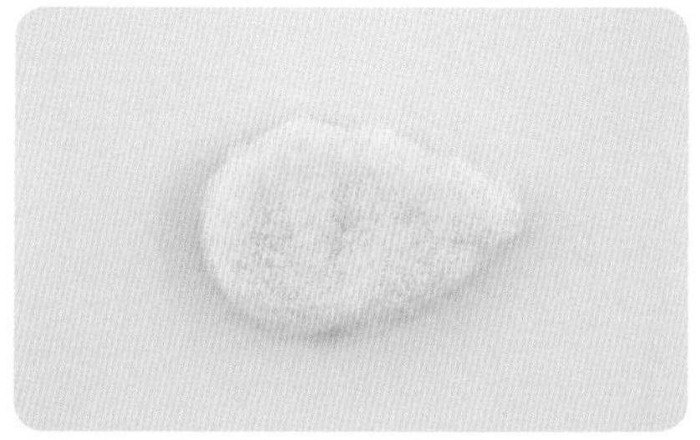

21 Remove the tape. The base for the wing is now complete.

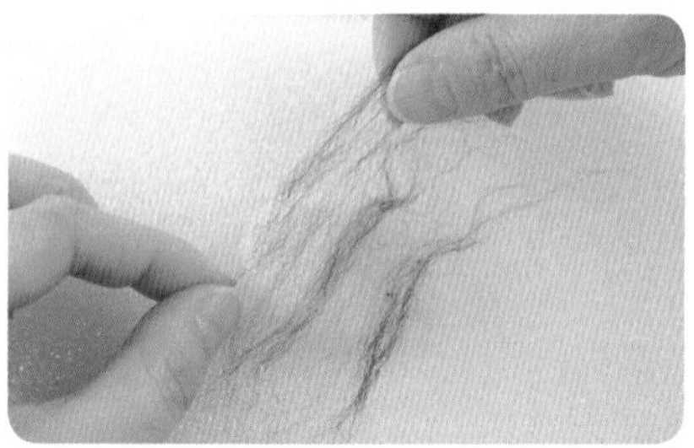

22 Loosen some black wool into thin wisps and place them over the wing in strips.

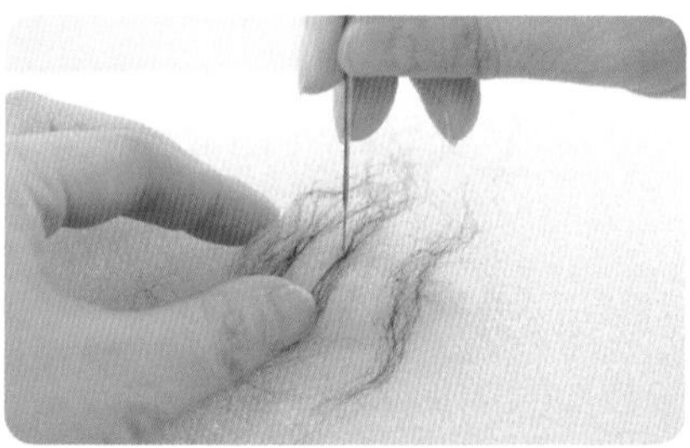

23 Felt in place with the needle.

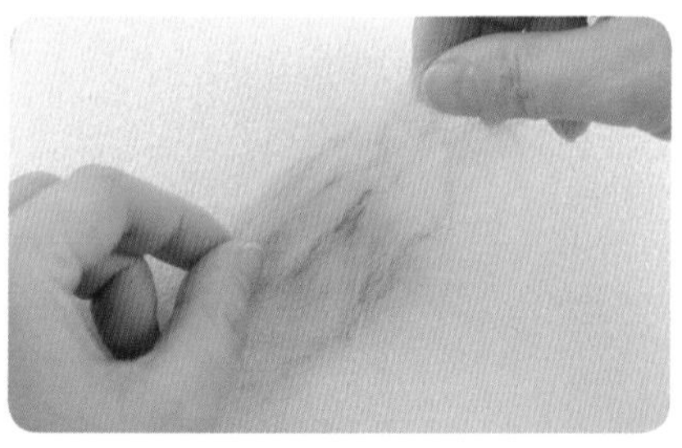

24 Now thinly loosen out some yellow-green into thin wisps and spread it over the entire wing.

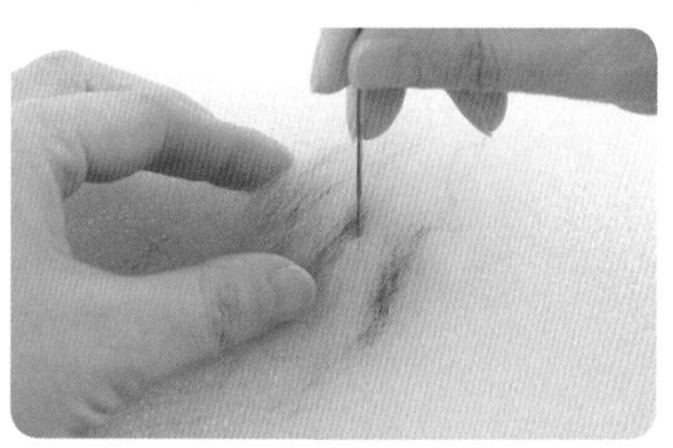

25 Felt in place with the needle.

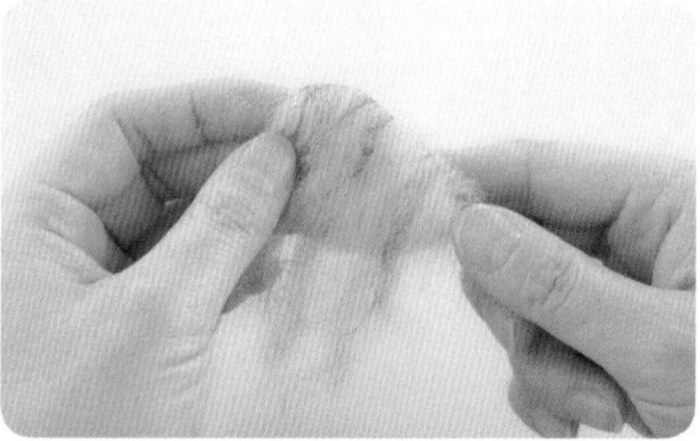

26 Fold the ends of the wool that you've spread over the wing round onto the reverse.

27 Felt in place from the front.
* Be careful with this step, as the wool will come out through the front if you jab it from the reverse.

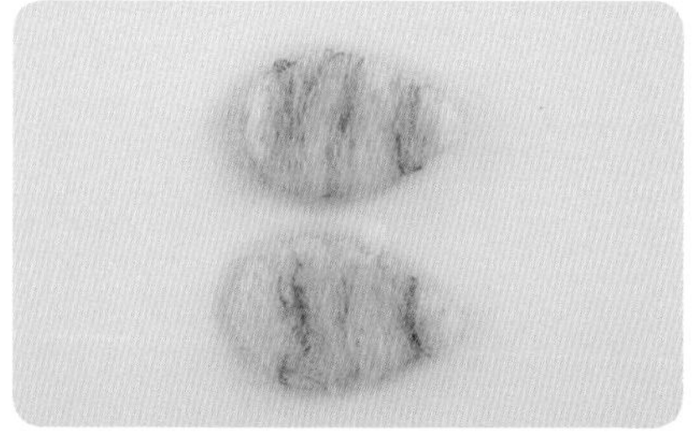

28 This how the wings look when complete. Make the second wing in the same way so that the two wings are left-right symmetrical.

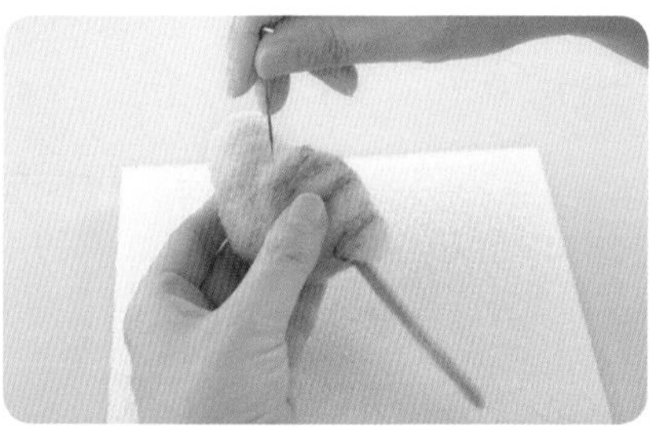

29 Needle felt the wings onto each side of the body.
Make sure that you felt the entire wing thoroughly.

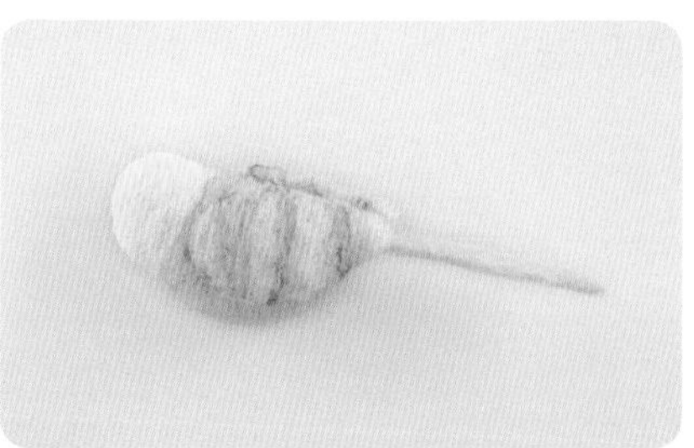

30 The wings are now attached.

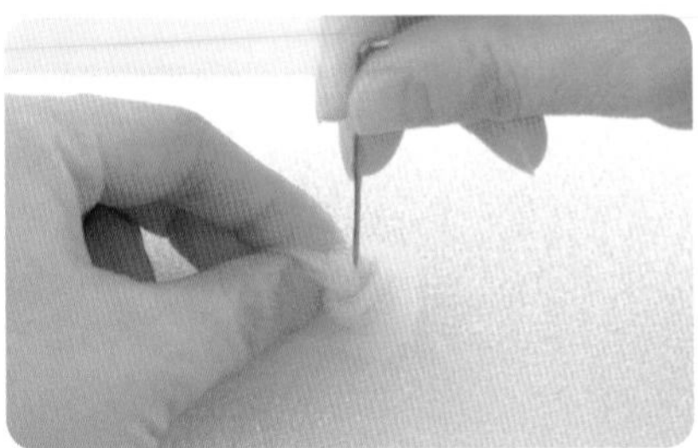

31 Make the beak.
Roll up a small amount of beige wool and felt it with the needle.

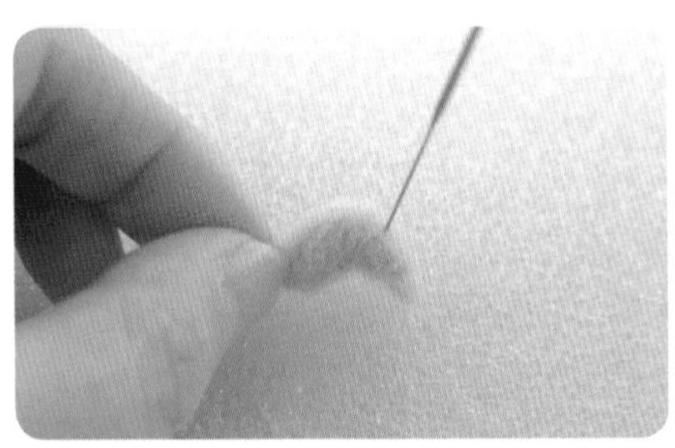

32 Use the actual-size component on p.41 to help you work it into something close to the right shape. Make it into a cashew-nut shape.

33 This is how the beak looks on completion.

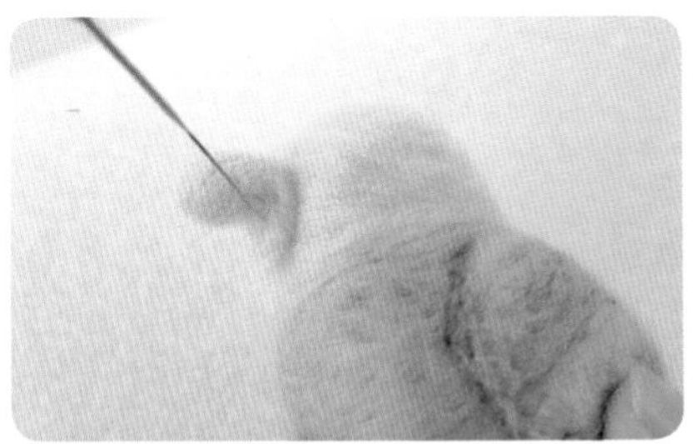

34 Felt the narrower end onto the head.

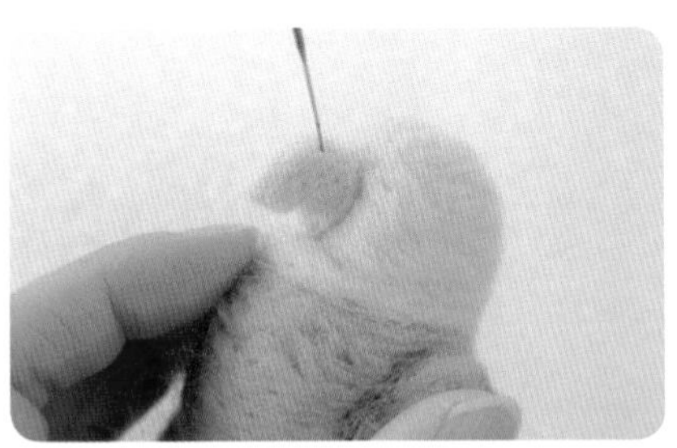

35 Also felt on the fat end, working from above.

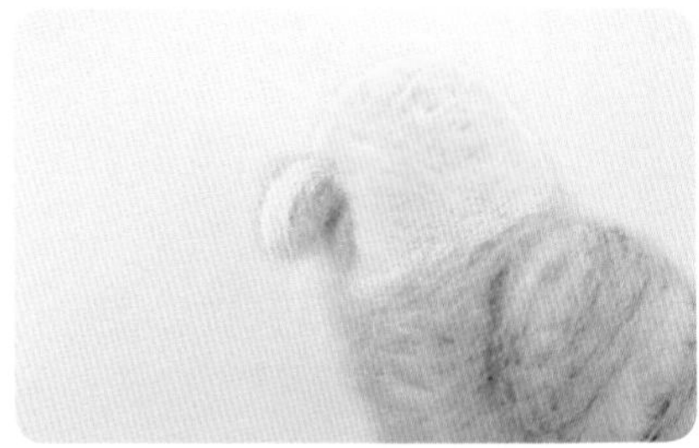

36 The beak is now attached.

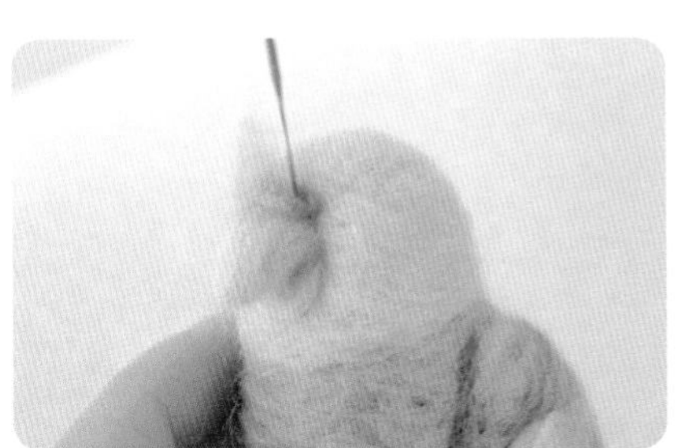

37 Take a small amount of saxe blue wool and felt it onto the top of the beak.

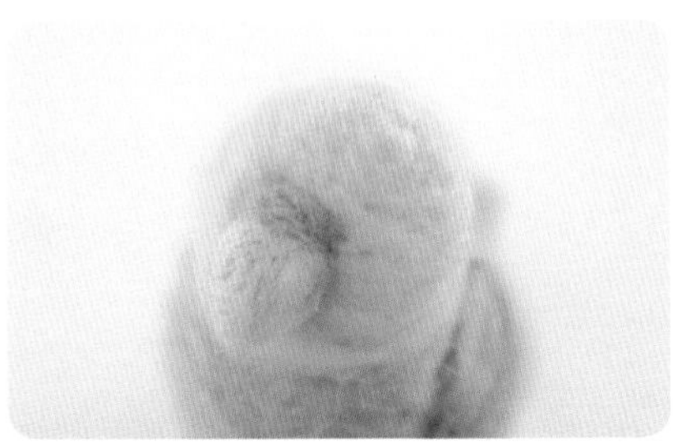

38 This is how it looks when done.

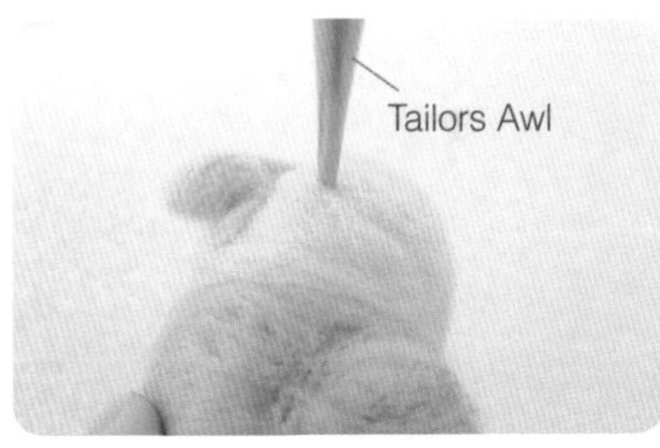
Tailors Awl

39 Make the face.
Use a tailor's awl to make a hole where the eye will go.

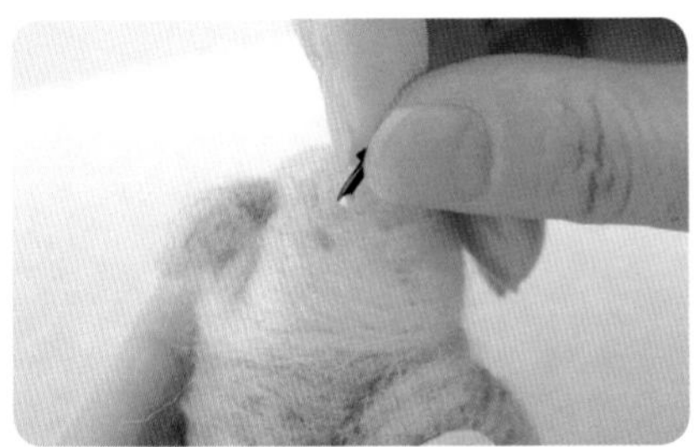

40 Dab some glue onto the solid eye and insert it into the hole.

41 The eye is now attached. Attach the other eye in the same way.

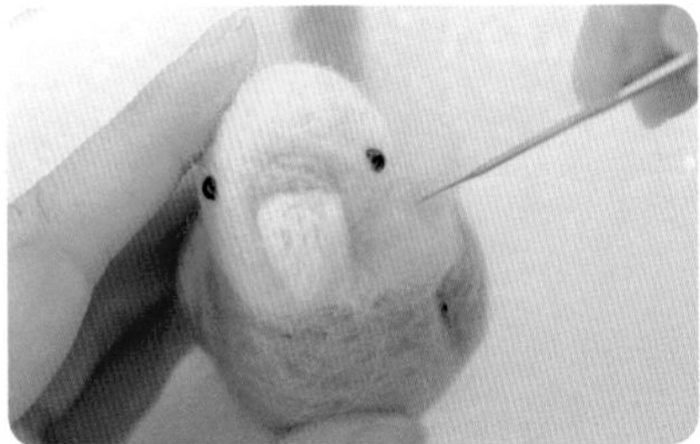

42 Take a small amount of custard wool and felt it onto the cheeks to puff them out.

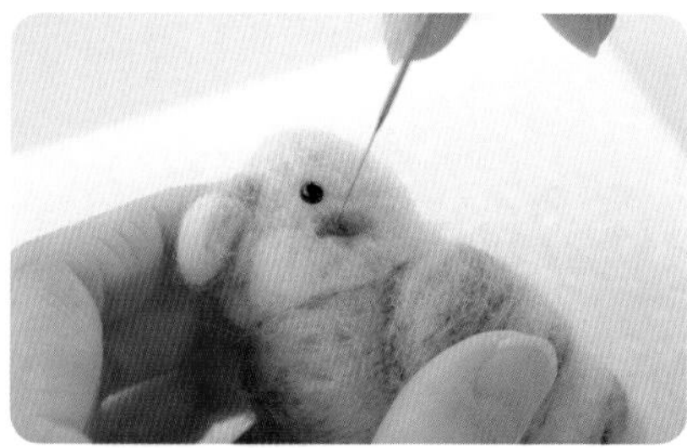

43 Felt a small amount of violet-blue wool under the eyes to add some patterning.

44 Felt on some patterning at two more points.

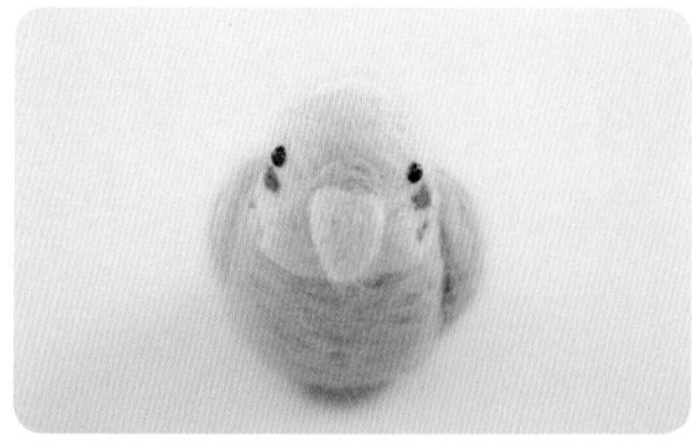

45 The face is now complete.

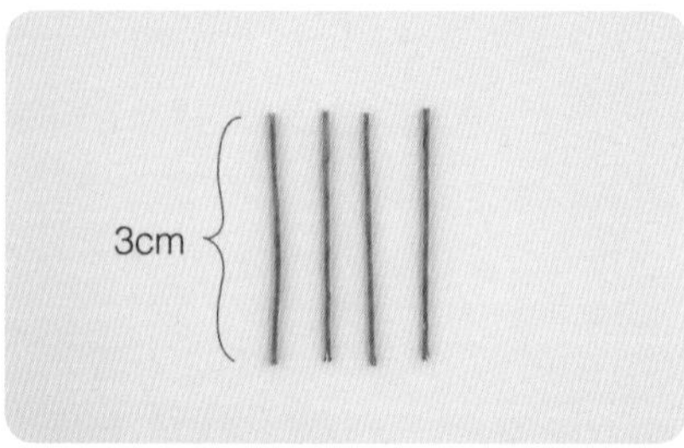
3cm

46 Make the legs.
Have ready four lengths of floral wire cut to 3 cm.

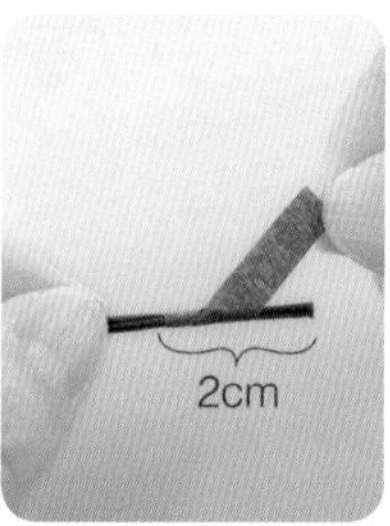
2cm

47 Group the four lengths together and wrap a 2-cm section of them in floral tape to hold them in place. Open out the wires of the remaining 1 cm into the shape of a foot with toes.

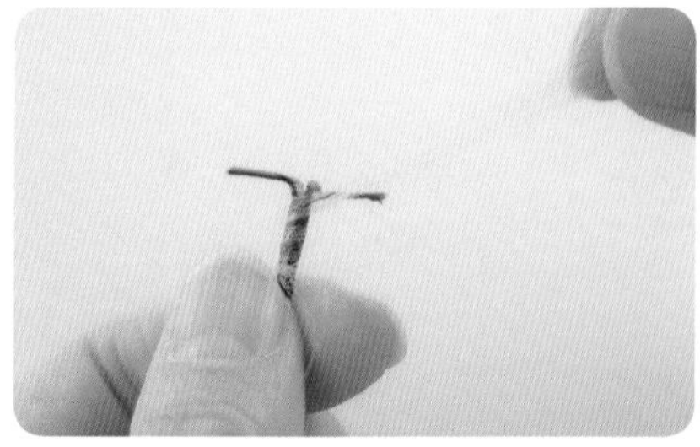

48 Take a small amount of light-pink wool and wind it round the wire. Floral tape is adhesive, so it will stick on by itself.

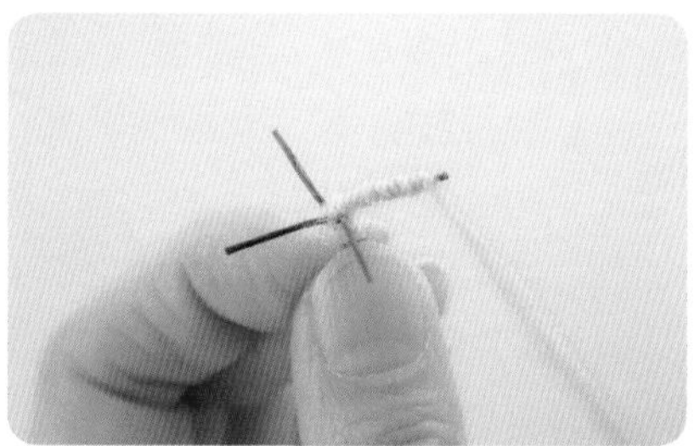

49 Keep going until you've also wound it onto the toes. Leave the claw part at the end of the toes bare.

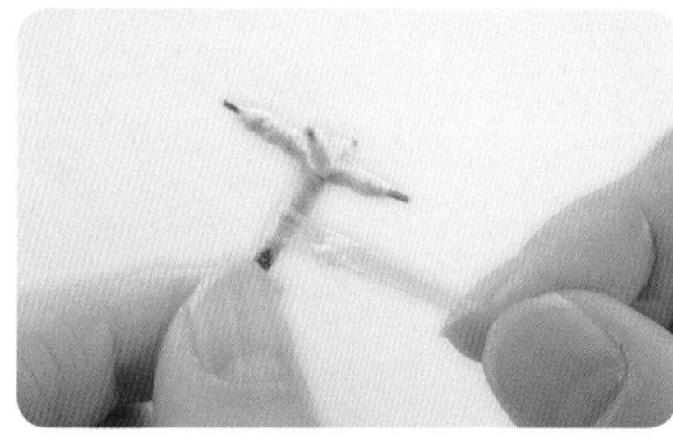

50 Dab a small amount of glue onto the end of the wool to hold it in place.

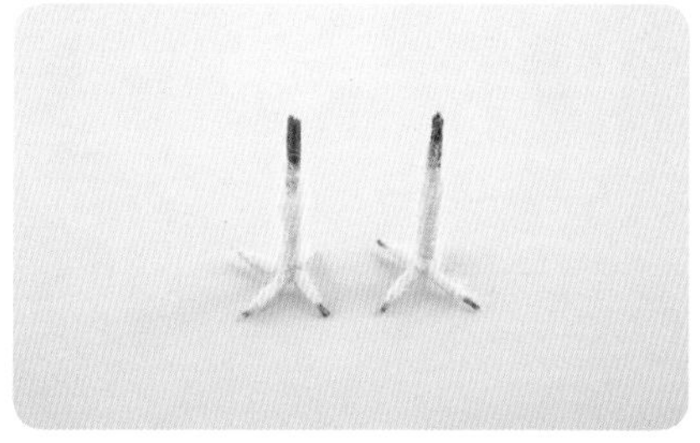

51 The leg is now complete. Make the other one in the same way.

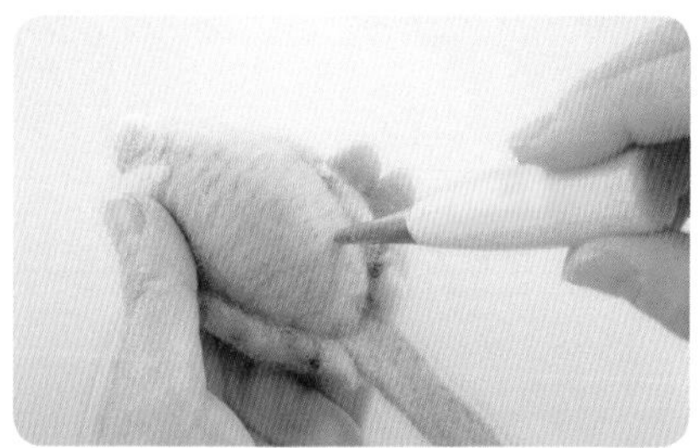

52 Use a tailor's awl to make holes where the legs will go.

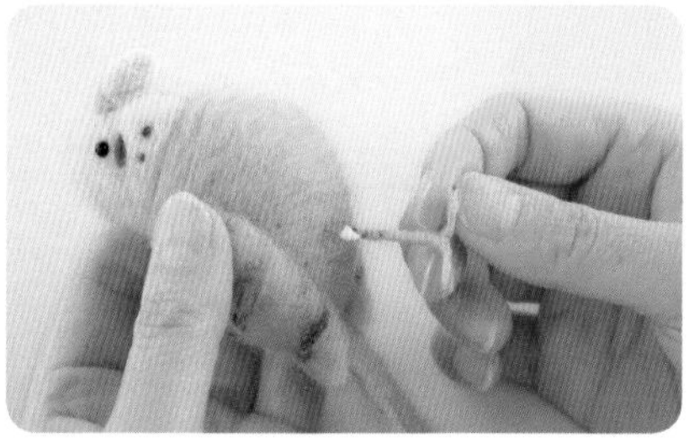

53 Dab some glue onto the legs and insert them into the holes.

54 This is how it looks on completion.

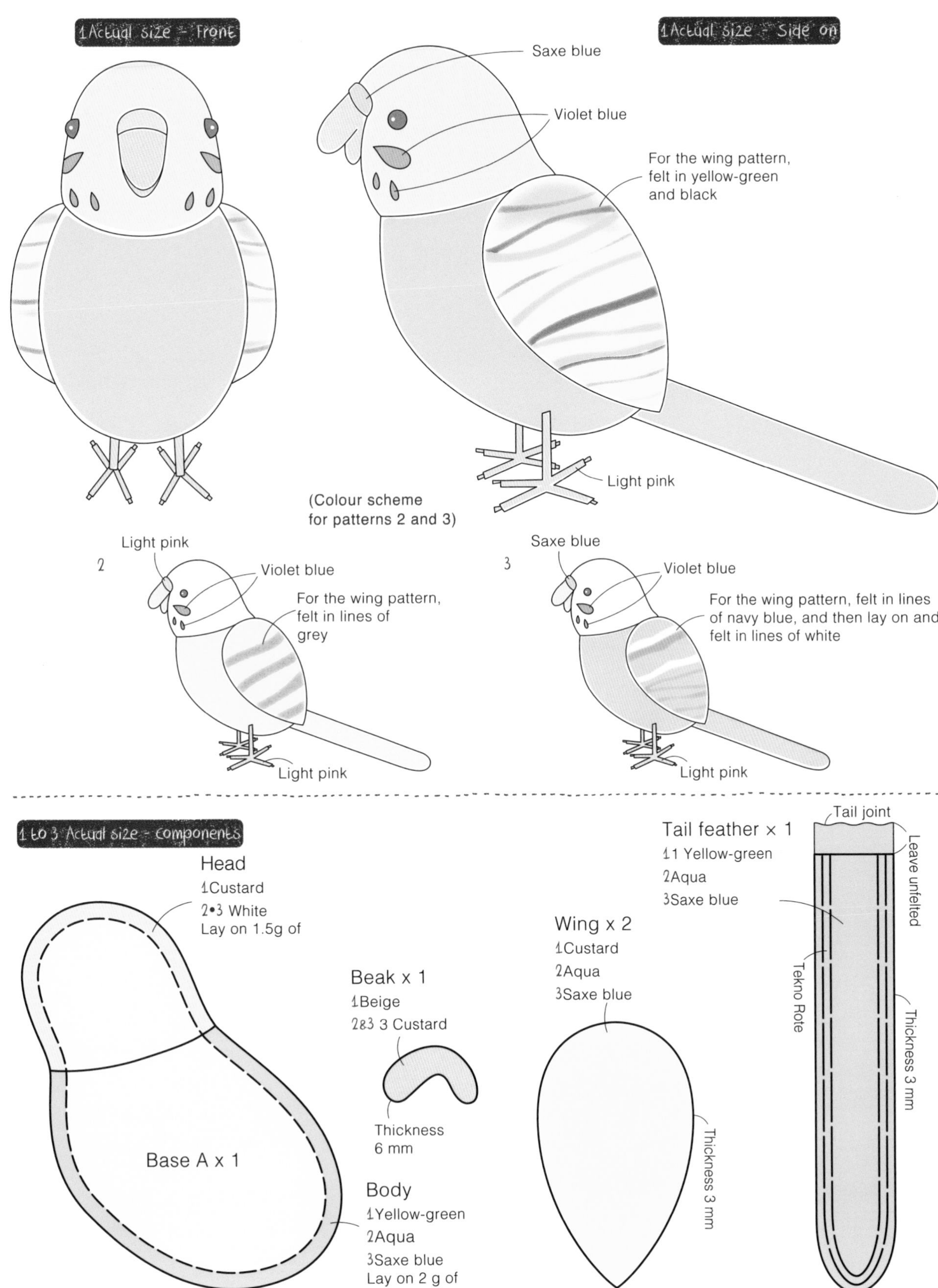
1 Actual size - Front
1 Actual size - Side on
Saxe blue
Violet blue
For the wing pattern, felt in yellow-green and black
Light pink
(Colour scheme for patterns 2 and 3)
2
Light pink
Violet blue
For the wing pattern, felt in lines of grey
Light pink
3
Saxe blue
Violet blue
For the wing pattern, felt in lines of navy blue, and then lay on and felt in lines of white
Light pink
1 to 3 Actual size - components
Head
1Custard
2•3 White
Lay on 1.5g of
Base A x 1
Beak x 1
1Beige
2&3 3 Custard
Thickness 6 mm
Body
1Yellow-green
2Aqua
3Saxe blue
Lay on 2 g of
Wing x 2
1Custard
2Aqua
3Saxe blue
Thickness 3 mm
Tail feather x 1
1 1 Yellow-green
2Aqua
3Saxe blue
Tail joint
Leave unfelted
Tekno Rote
Thickness 3 mm

Rosy faced love bird

number 33 on page 28

Materials

Felt wool

Solid
- •Moss green, 1 g
- •Light pink
- •Golden yellow
- •Dark green small amounts

Natural Blend
- •Red, small amount

Solid eye · 2 mm x 1

Other materials

- •Felt 5 cm × 5 cm
- •Brooch pin (20 mm) x 1

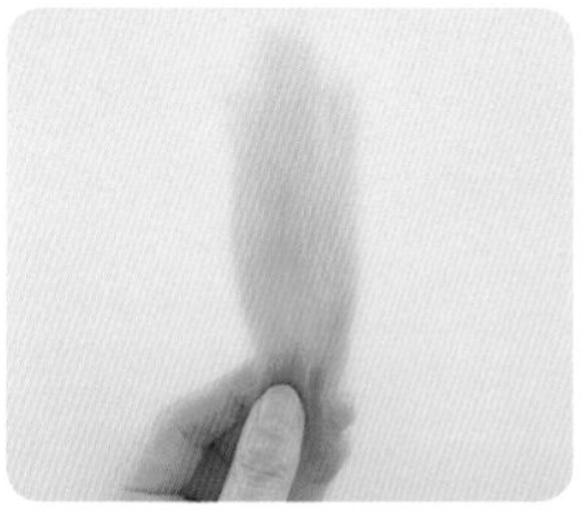

1 Make the body. Tear off some moss-green wool and take a small amount of it.

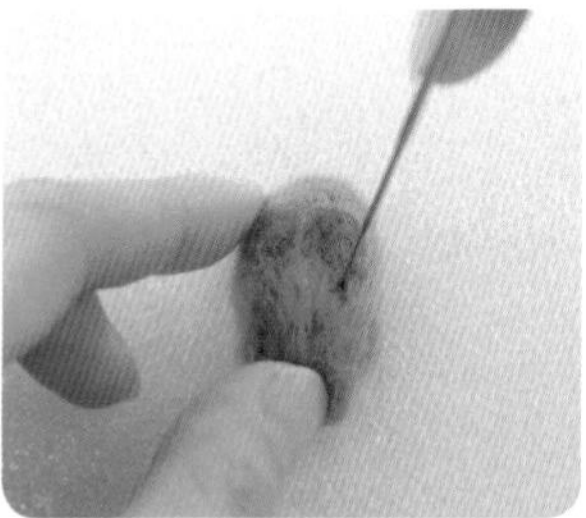

2 Roll the wool up and jab it with the needle, working towards the shape of the actual-sized component.

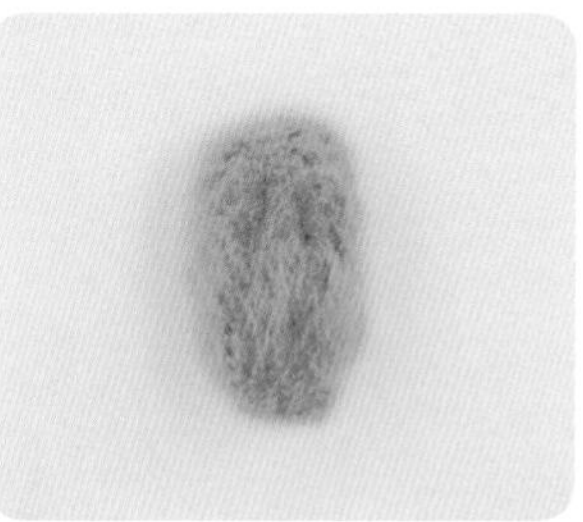

3 This is how the body looks on completion.

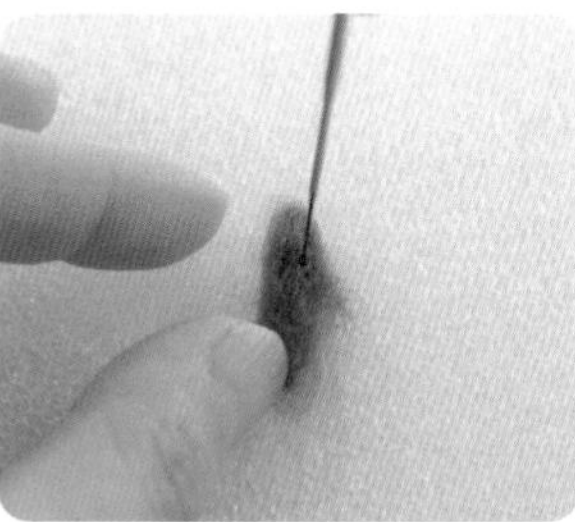

4 Make the tail feather. Roll up a small amount of dark green wool and felt it into a long, thin shape.

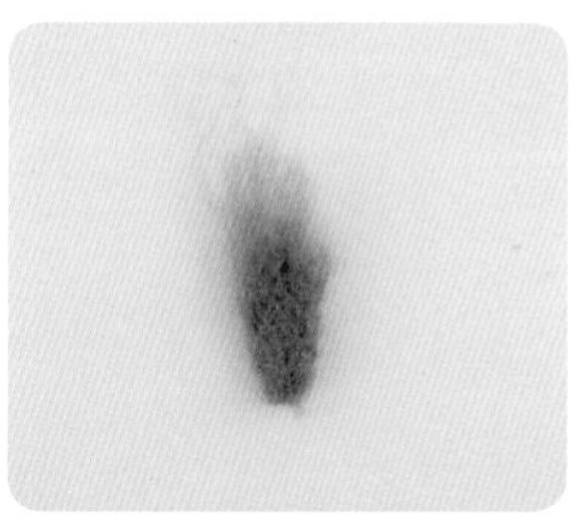

5 This is how the tail feather looks on completion. Leave the area at the base of the tail wispy, without stabbing it.

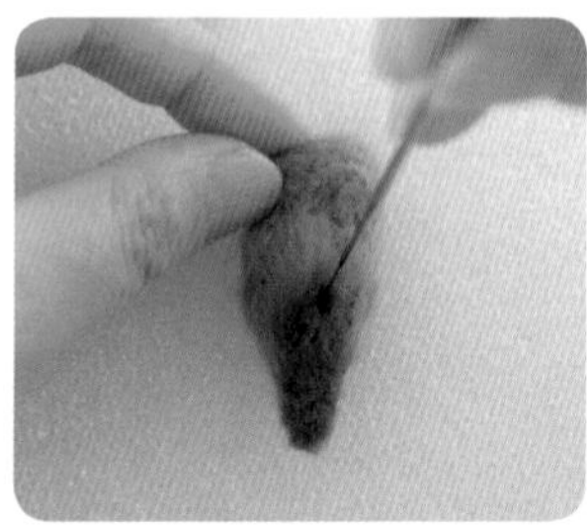

6 Felt the tail feather onto the body.

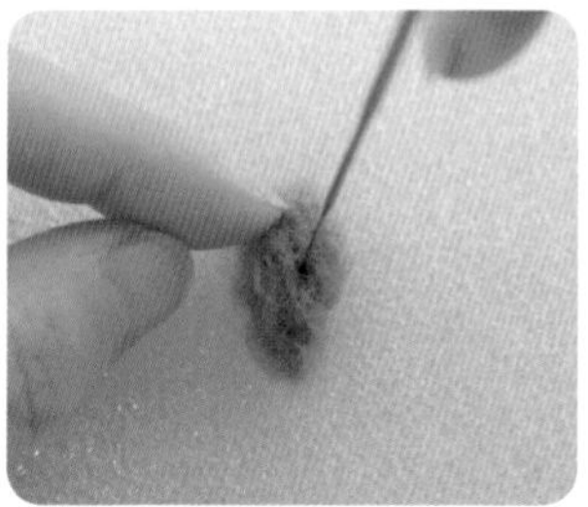

7 Make the wings from moss-green wool in the same way.

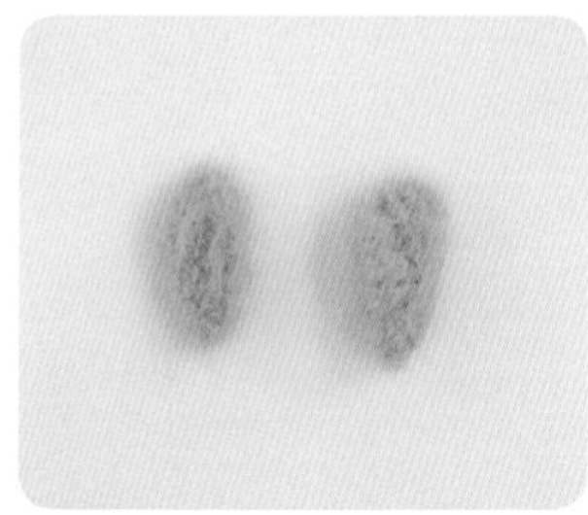

8 This is how the wings look when complete.

9 Felt the wings onto the body.

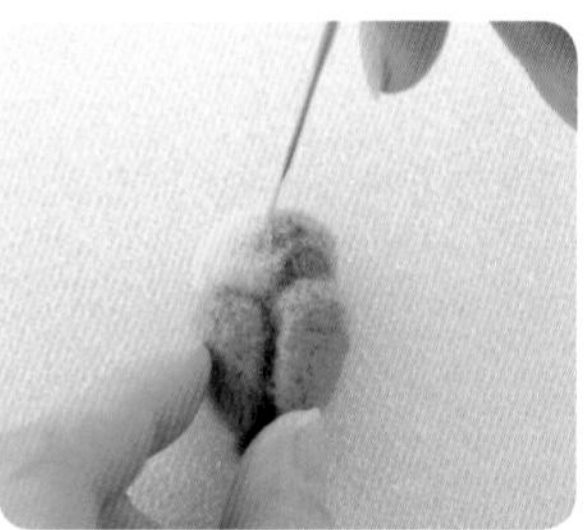

10 Place a small amount of light-pink wool on the face area and felt it with the needle.

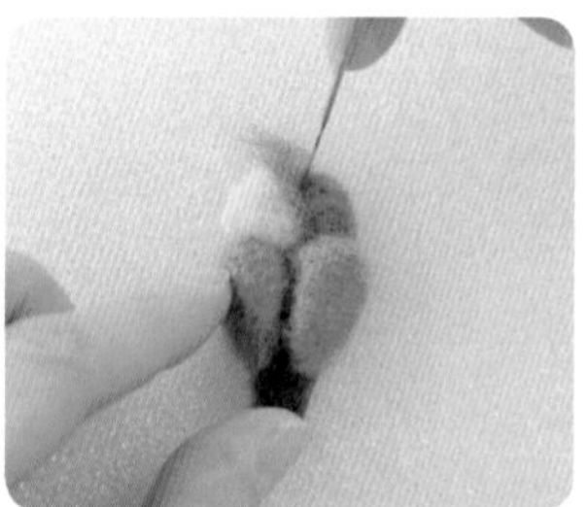

11 Lay some red wool over the top part of the face and felt it with the needle.

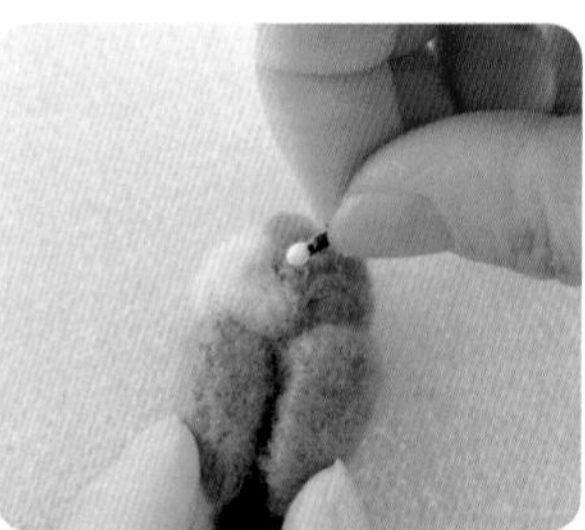

12 Use a tailor's awl to make a hole where the eye will go and insert the solid eye with a dab of glue on it.

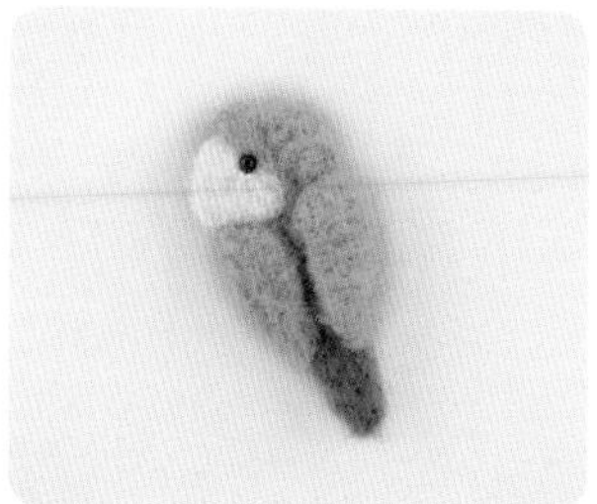

13 The eye is now attached.

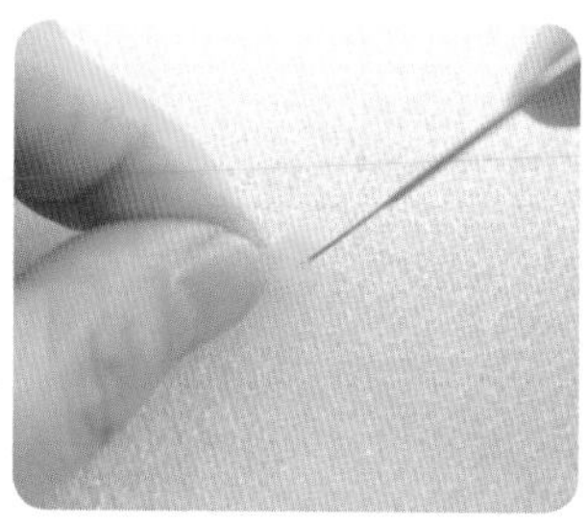

14 Roll up a small amount of golden yellow wool and felt it with the needle to form the beak.

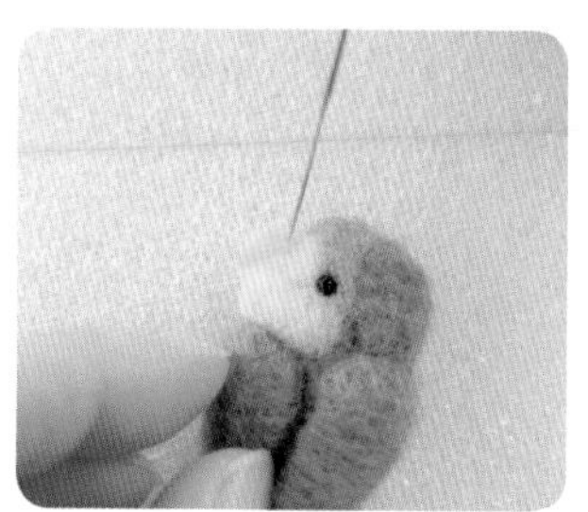

15 Felt the beak onto the face.

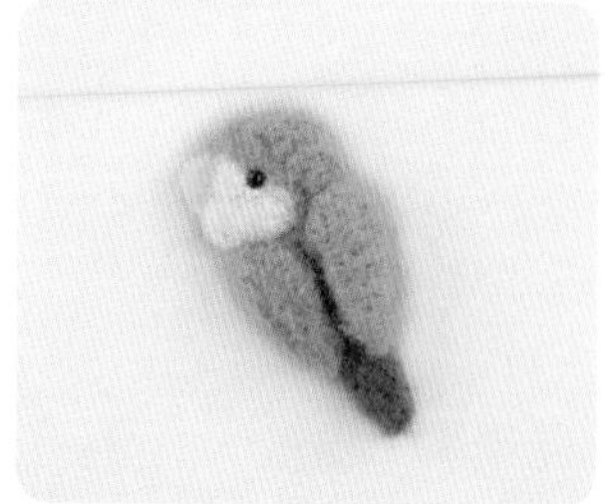

16 The beak is now attached. This is how the rosy-faced lovebird looks on completion.

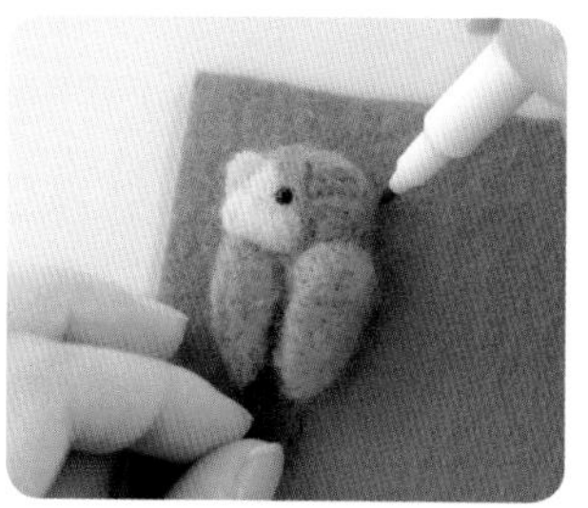

17 Make the backing patch. Place the parrot on the felt and trace its outline with an air-soluble marker.

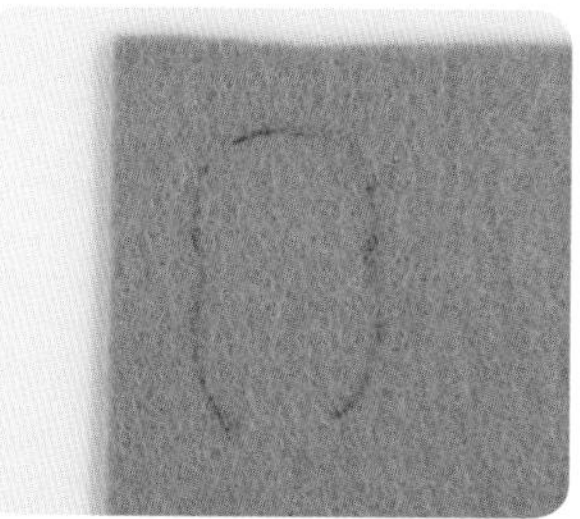

18 You don't need to draw the tail feather section.

19 Cut out the area inside the lines with a pair of scissors.

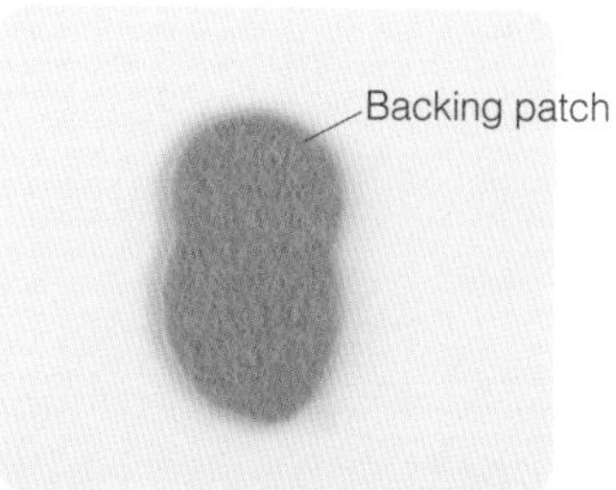
Backing patch

20 The backing patch is now complete.

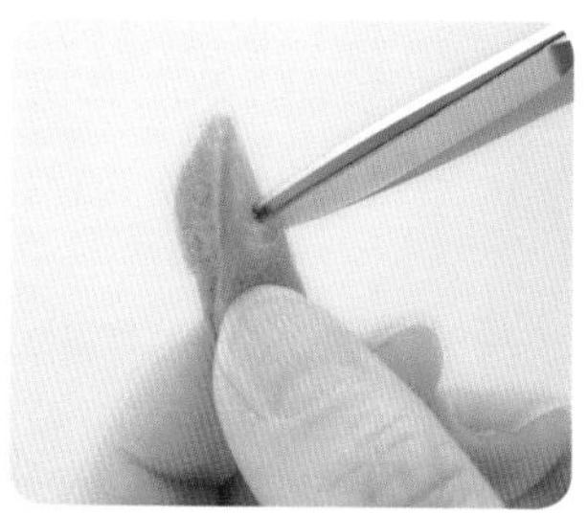

21 Make a snips in the backing patch to fit the size of the brooch pin.

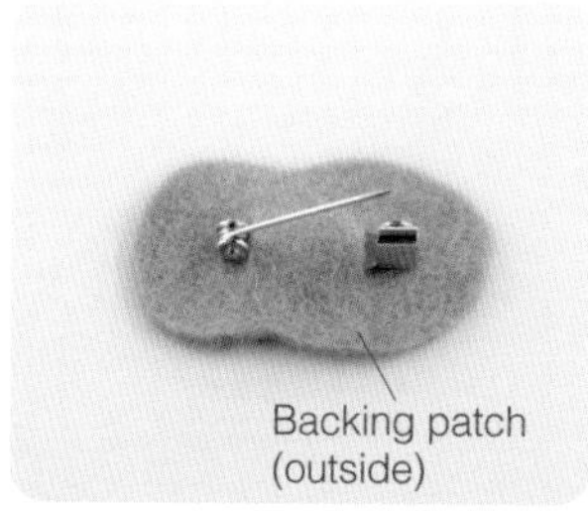
Backing patch
(outside)

22 Slide the brooch pin through.

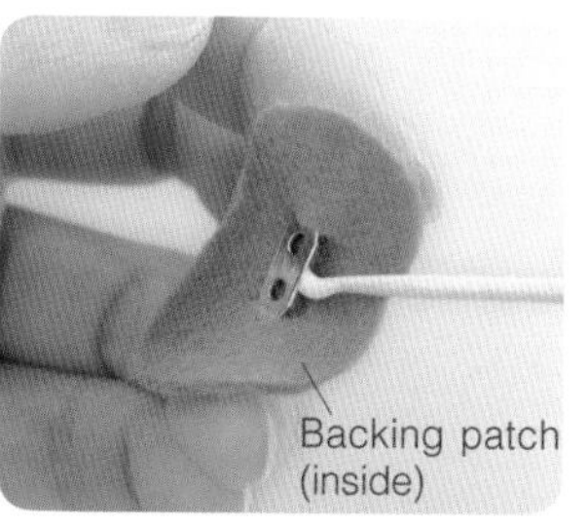
Backing patch
(inside)

23 Add some glue to the back of the brooch pin to stick it onto the felt.

24 Glue the entire surface of the inside of the backing patch and stick it onto the back of the model.

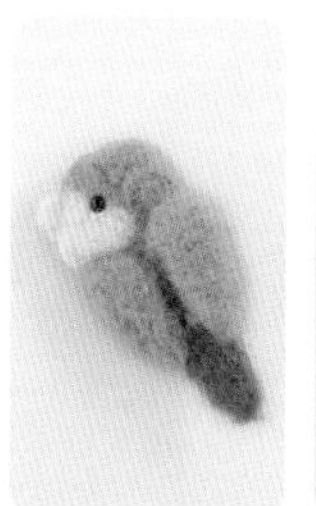

25 This is how the brooch looks on completion.

Actual size - Front

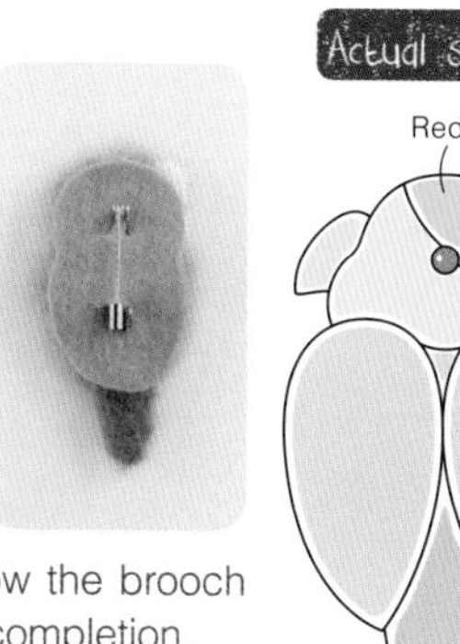
Red
Light pink

Actual size - Components

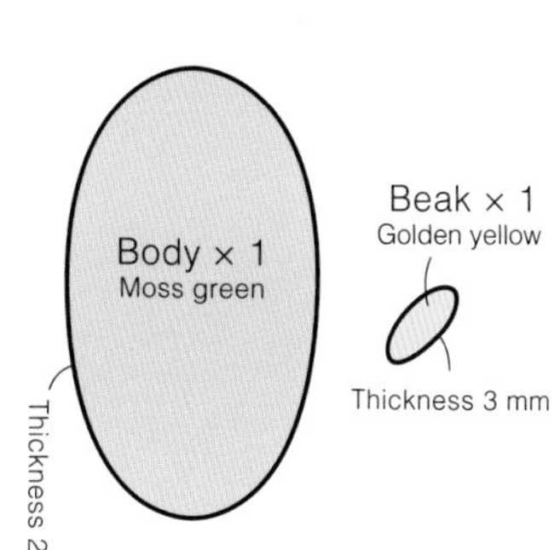
Body × 1
Moss green
Thickness 2 mm
Beak × 1
Golden yellow
Thickness 3 mm

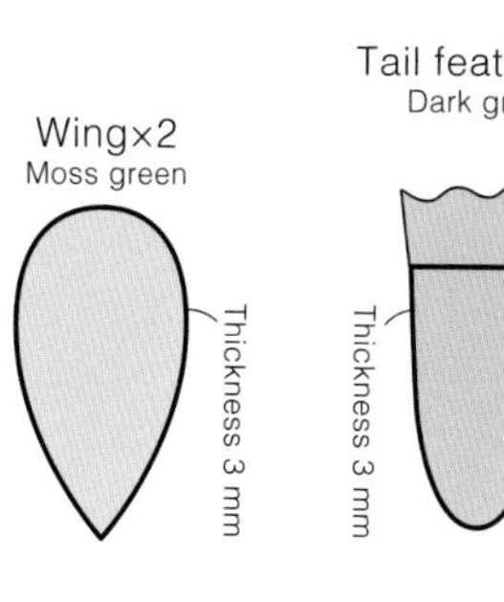
Wing×2
Moss green
Thickness 3 mm
Tail feather×1
Dark green
Tail joint
Leave unfelted
Thickness 3 mm

4 & 5 Cockatiel

Materials for 4

Felt wool

Solid
- •Off-white, 4 g
- •Cream, 2.5 g
- •Bitter orange
- •Light pink, small amounts

Natural Blend
- •Undyed, small amount

Mix
- •Grey, 6 g

Solid eyes •4 mm x 2

Other materials
- •Clear plastic wallet 2 cm × 13 cm
- •Floral wire (brown, 24 gauge) 8 x 3-cm lengths
- •Tekno Rote 16 cm
- •Floral tape, amount to suit

Materials for 5

Felt wool

Solid
- •Off-white, 4 g
- •Cream, 2.5 g
- •Bitter orange
- •Light pink), small amounts

Natural Blend
- •Undyed, 6 g

Mix amount •Grey small

Solid eyes • 4 mm x 2

Other materials
- •Clear plastic wallet 2 cm × 13 cm
- •Floral wire (brown, 24 gauge) 8 x 3-cm lengths
- •Tekno Rote 16 cm
- •Floral tape, amount to suit

Instructions

For basic instructions to help you make the birds,see pp.34 to 40.

1 Make the base.

2 Felt the wool of the head and body onto the base.

3 Make and attach the tail feather.

4 Make and attach the wings

5 Make and attach the crest.

6 Make and attach the beak.

7 Make the face.

8 Make and attach the legs

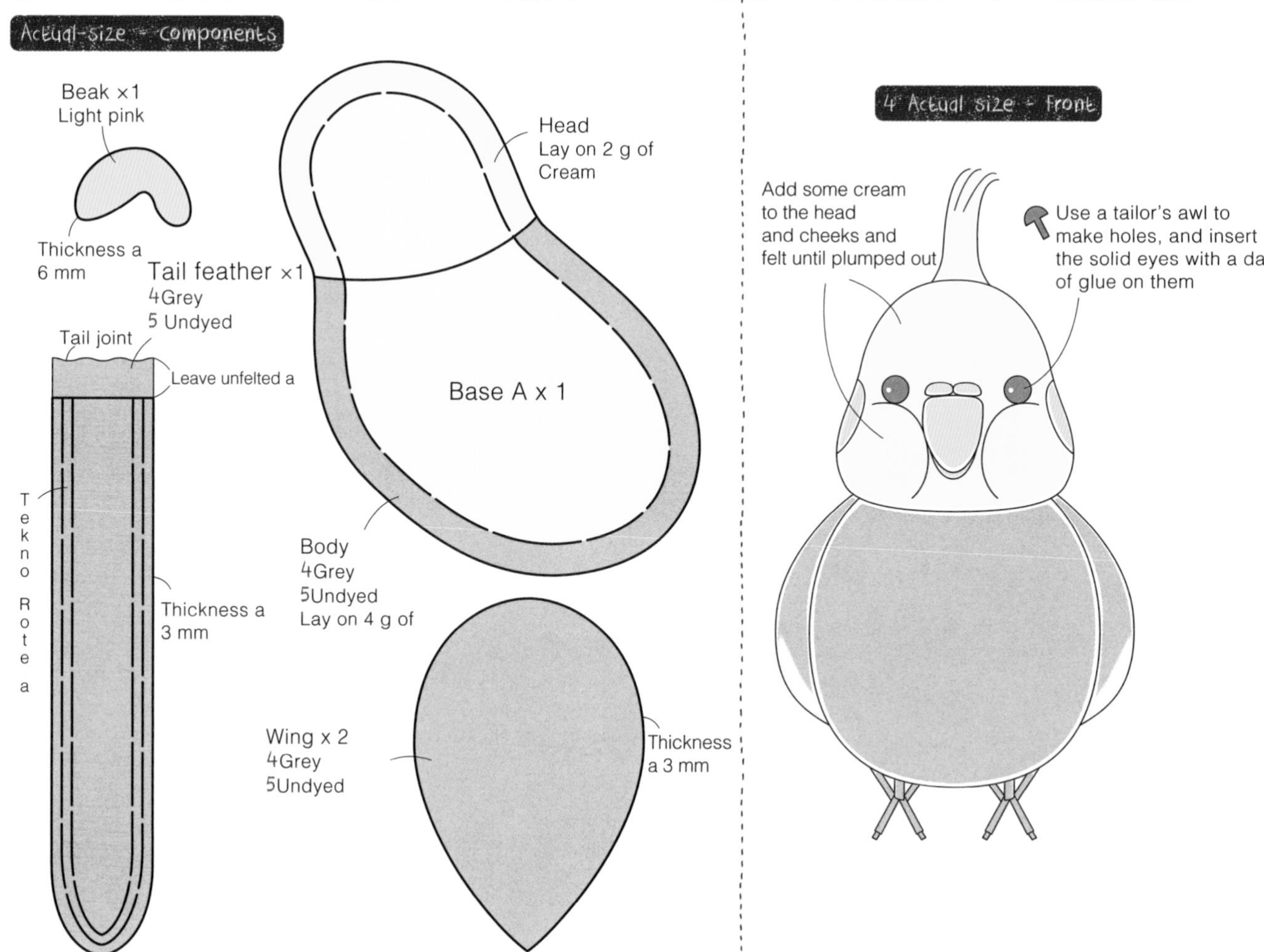

Actual-size components
Beak ×1
Light pink
Thickness a
6 mm
Tail feather ×1
4Grey
5 Undyed
Tail joint
Leave unfelted a
Tekno Rote a
Thickness a
3 mm
Head
Lay on 2 g of
Cream
Base A x 1
Body
4Grey
5Undyed
Lay on 4 g of
Wing x 2
4Grey
5Undyed
Thickness
a 3 mm
4 Actual size - front
Add some cream
to the head
and cheeks and
felt until plumped out
Use a tailor's awl to
make holes, and insert
the solid eyes with a dab
of glue on them

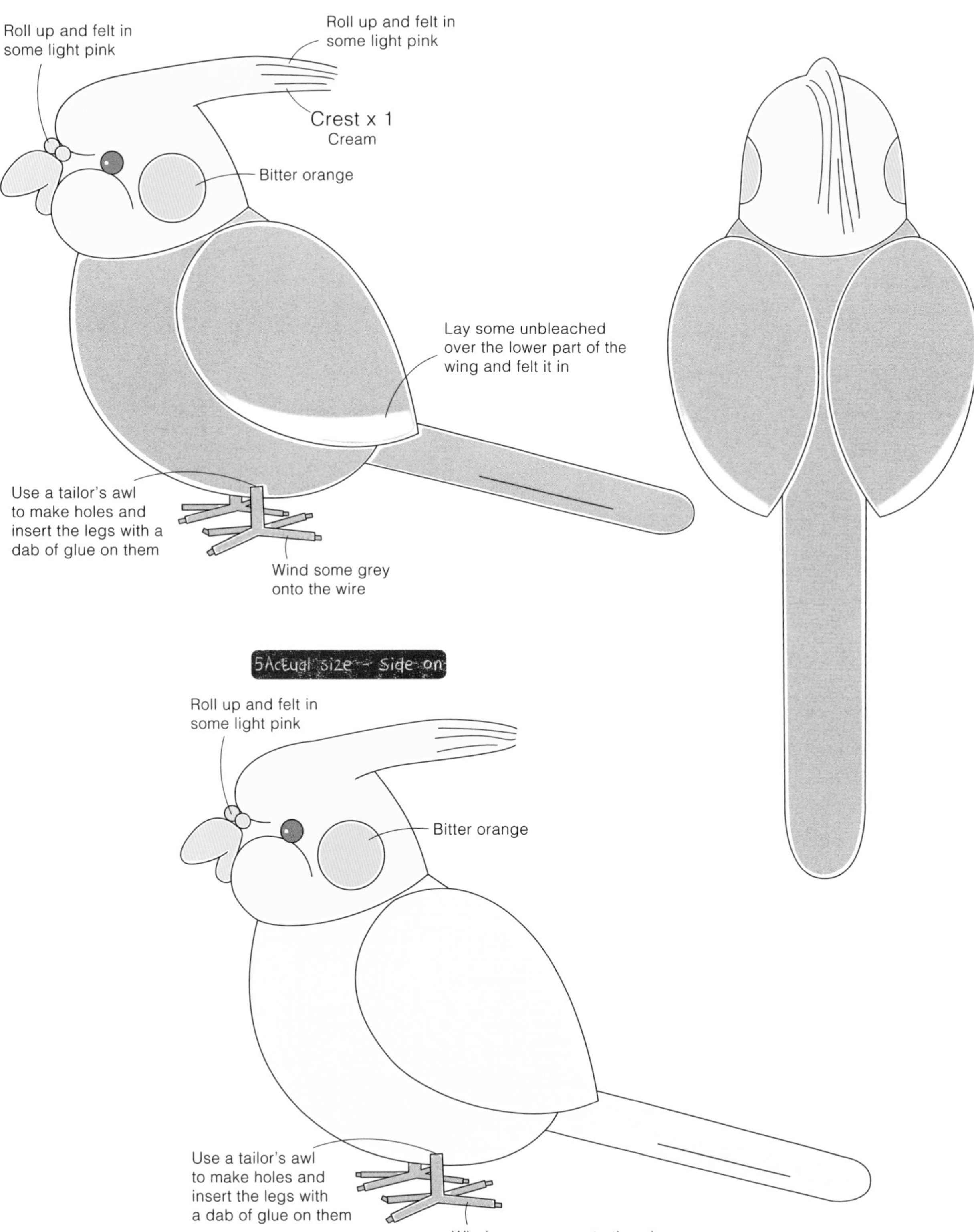
4 Actual size – Side on
Roll up and felt in some light pink
Roll up and felt in some light pink
Crest x 1
Cream
Bitter orange
Lay some unbleached over the lower part of the wing and felt it in
Use a tailor's awl to make holes and insert the legs with a dab of glue on them
Wind some grey onto the wire
4 Actual size – Back
5 Actual size – Side on
Roll up and felt in some light pink
Bitter orange
Use a tailor's awl to make holes and insert the legs with a dab of glue on them
Wind some grey onto the wire

6 Rosy-faced Lovebird

Materials (for one bird)

Felt wool

Solid
- •Off-white, 4 g
- •Moss green, 3 g • Fresh leaf, 2 g
- •Light pink • Dark green, small amounts

Natural Blend
- •Cream • Cerulean blue
- •Red • Beige grey, small amounts

Solid eyes • 3.5 mm x 2

Other materials
- •Clear plastic wallet 2 cm × 12 cm
- •Floral wire (brown, 24 gauge) 8 x 3-cm lengths
- •Tekno Rote 8 cm
- •Floral tape, amount to suit

Instructions

For basic instructions to help you make the birds, see pp.34 to 40.

1 Make the base.

2 Felt the wool of the head and body onto the base.

3 Lay the wool indicated in the instructions over the head and body and then felt it on.

4 Make and attach the tail feathers.

5 Make and attach the wings.

6 Make and attach the beak.

7 Make the face.

8 Make and attach the legs.

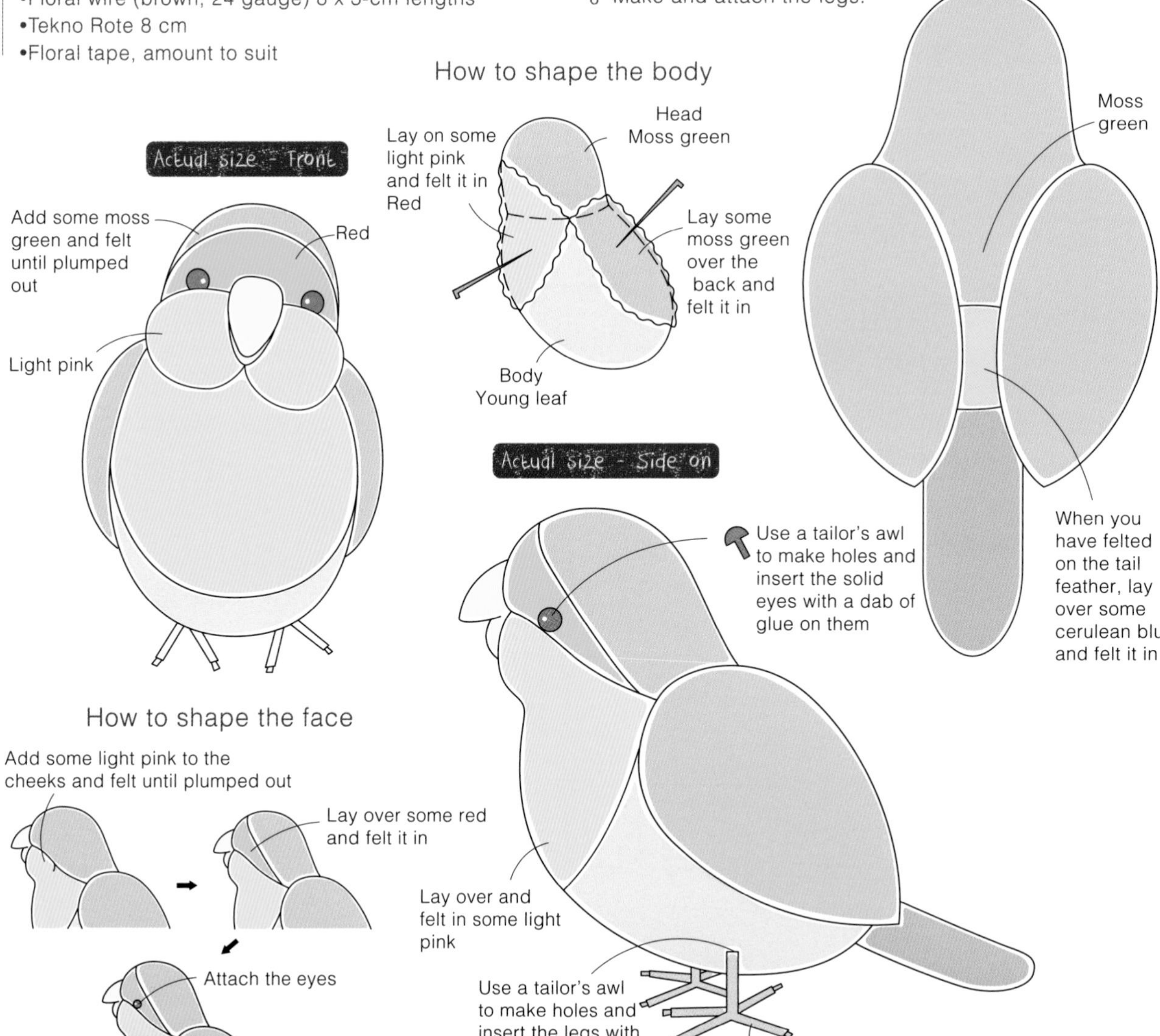

Actual size - Back
Moss green
When you have felted on the tail feather, lay over some cerulean blue and felt it in
How to shape the body
Head
Moss green
Lay on some light pink and felt it in
Red
Lay some moss green over the back and felt it in
Body
Young leaf
Actual size - Front
Add some moss green and felt until plumped out
Red
Light pink
Actual size - Side on
Use a tailor's awl to make holes and insert the solid eyes with a dab of glue on them
How to shape the face
Add some light pink to the cheeks and felt until plumped out
Lay over some red and felt it in
Attach the eyes
Lay over and felt in some light pink
Use a tailor's awl to make holes and insert the legs with a dab of glue on them
Wind some beige-grey onto the wire

6 Actual-size - components

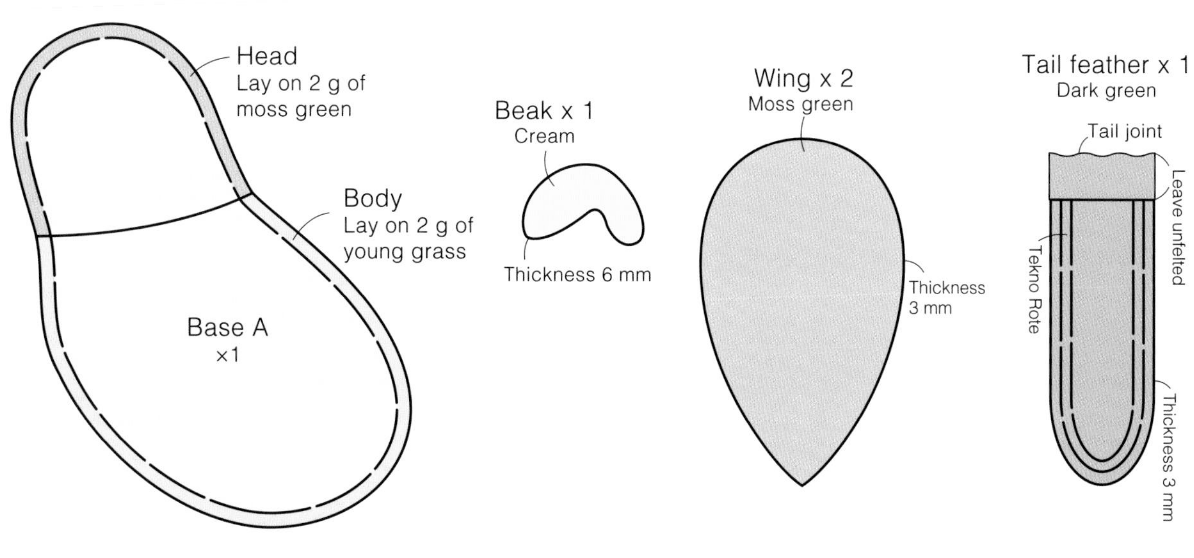
Head
Lay on 2 g of moss green
Body
Lay on 2 g of young grass
Base A
×1
Beak x 1
Cream
Thickness 6 mm
Wing x 2
Moss green
Thickness 3 mm
Tail feather x 1
Dark green
Tail joint
Leave unfelted
Tekno Rote
Thickness 3 mm

7 Actual-size - components

Wing tip A x 2
Black
Wing-tip joint
Thickness 2 mm

Wing tip B x 2
Black
Wing-tip joint
Thickness 2 mm

Wing tip C x 2
Black
Wing-tip joint
Thickness 2 mm

Crest A x 2
Pale pink
Slit
Thickness 2 mm
Leave unfelted

Crest B x 1
Pale pink
Slit
Thickness 2 mm
Leave unfelted
Crest joint

Tail feather A x 1
Grey
Tail joint
Leave unfelted
Tekno Rote 14 cm
Thickness 3 mm

Tail feather B x 2
Grey
Tail joint
Leave unfelted
Tekno Rote 13 cm
Thickness 3 mm

Beak x 1
Light beige
Thickness 6 mm

Head
Pale pink
Lay on 3

Body
Lay on 3 g of Pink

Base A
×1

Wing x 2
Grey
Thickness 3 mm

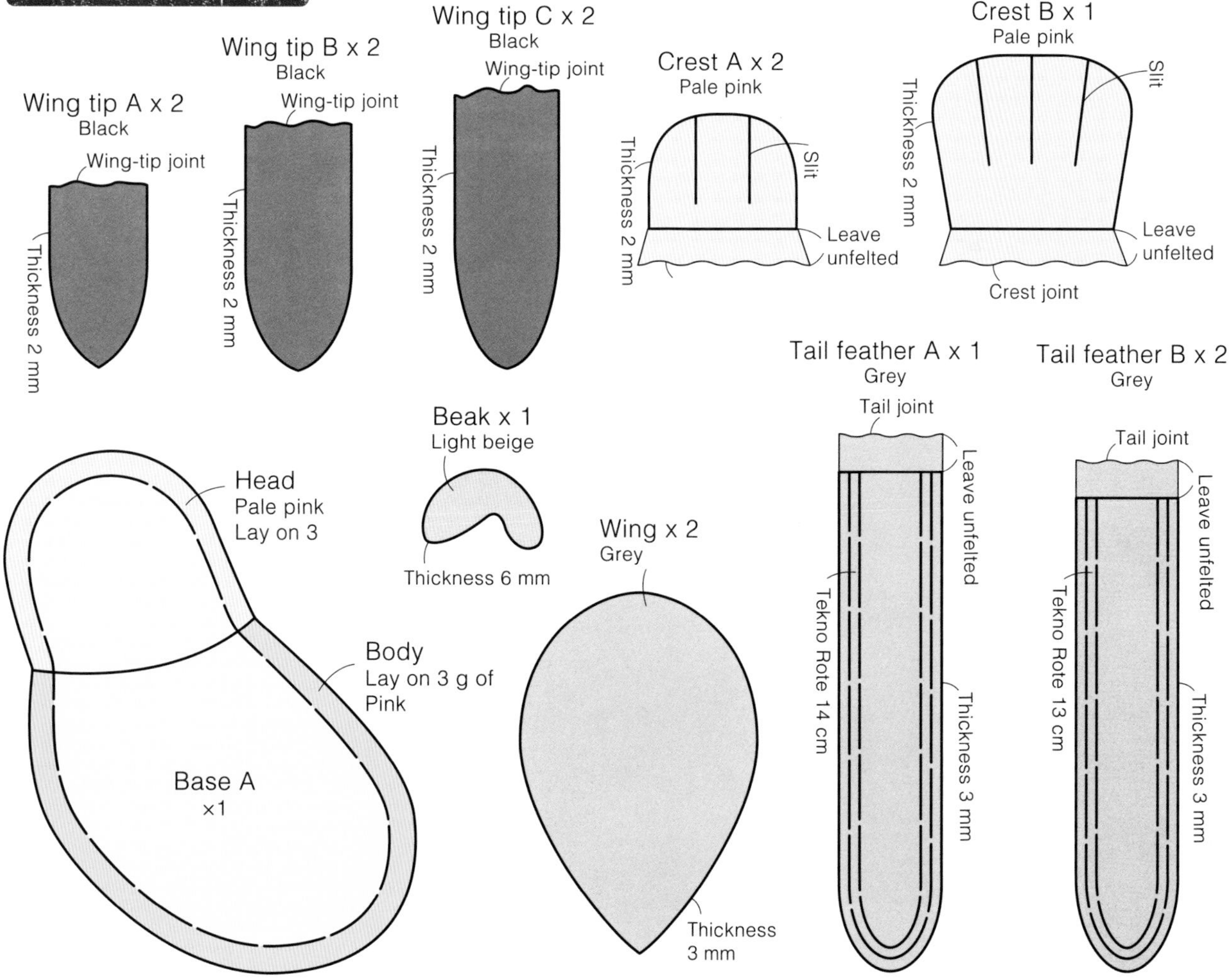

Page 9

7 Galah

Materials

Felt wool

Solid	•Off-white, 4 g •Pale pink,4 g •Dark pink small amount
Natural Blend	•Pink,5 g •Grey, 4 g •Light beige, small amount
Mix	•Black, 1 g

Solid eyes • 4 mm x 2 mm x 2

Other materials

- •Clear plastic wallet 2 cm×13 cm
- •Floral wire (brown, 24 gauge) 8×3 cm lengths
- •Tekno Rote 40 cm
- •Floral tape, amount to suit

※The actual-size components are on p.47

Instructions

※For basic instructions to help you make the birds, see pp.34 to 40.

1 Make the base.
2 Felt the wool of the head and body onto the base.
3 Lay the wool indicated in the instructions over the head and body and felt it on.
4 Make and attach the tail feathers
5 Make and attach the wings
6 Make and attach the crest
7 Make and attach the beak
8 Make the face
9 Make and attach the legs

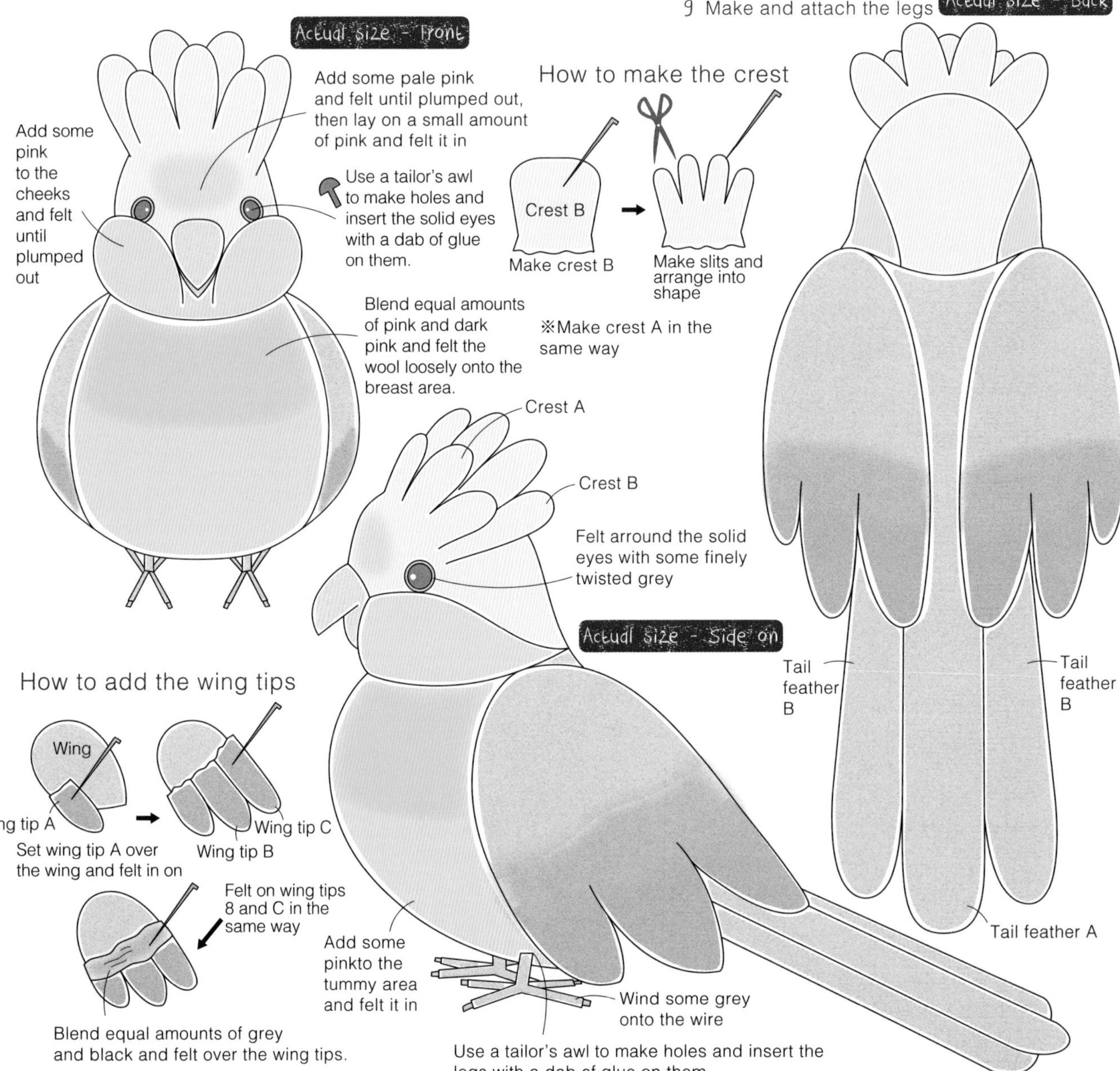

Actual size - Front
Add some pink to the cheeks and felt until plumped out
Add some pale pink and felt until plumped out, then lay on a small amount of pink and felt it in
Use a tailor's awl to make holes and insert the solid eyes with a dab of glue on them.
Blend equal amounts of pink and dark pink and felt the wool loosely onto the breast area.
How to make the crest
Crest B
Make crest B
Make slits and arrange into shape
※Make crest A in the same way
Actual size - Back
Crest A
Crest B
Felt arround the solid eyes with some finely twisted grey
Actual size - Side on
Tail feather B
Tail feather B
Tail feather A
How to add the wing tips
Wing
Wing tip A
Set wing tip A over the wing and felt in on
Wing tip B
Wing tip C
Felt on wing tips 8 and C in the same way
Blend equal amounts of grey and black and felt over the wing tips.
Add some pinkto the tummy area and felt it in
Wind some grey onto the wire
Use a tailor's awl to make holes and insert the legs with a dab of glue on them.

Page 10

8 & 9 Lilian's lovebird

Materials for 8

Felt wool

Solid
- •Off-white, 2 g
- •Aqua, 2 g
- •Dark brown, 2 g
- •White -Light pink, small amounts

Natural Blend
- •Cerulean blue, 1.5 g
- •Grey, small amount

Solid eyes • 4 mm x 2

Other materials
- •Clear plastic wallet 2 cm × 12 cm
- •Floral wire (brown, 24 gauge) 8 x 4-cm lengths
- •Tekno Rote 8 cm
- •Floral tape, amount to suit

Materials for 9

Felt wool

Solid
- •Off-white, 4 g
- •Young leaf, 2 g
- •Dark green, 1.5 g
- •White - Golden yellow
- •Vermilion
- •Lemon yellow, small amounts

Natural Blend
- •Beige grey, small amount

Max
- •Cinnamon brown, 2 g
- •Navy blue, small amount

Solid eyes • 4 mm x 2

Other materials
- •Clear plastic wallet 2 cm × 12 cm
- •Floral wire (brown, 24 gauge) 8 x 4-cm lengths
- •Tekno Rote 8 cm
- •Floral tape, amount to suit

※The actual-size components are on p.50.

Instructions

※For basic instructions to help you make the birds, see pp.34 to 40.

1. Make the base.
2. Felt the wool of the head and body onto the base.
3. Lay the wool indicated in the instructions over the head and body and then felt it on.
4. Make and attach the tail feather.
5. Make and attach the wings.
6. Make and attach the beak.
7. Make the face.
8. Make and attach the legs.

Actual size - Front

Felt some finely twisted white onto the top of the beak
8Grey
9Golden yellow
8White
9Lemon yellow
8Cerulean blue
9Dark green

How to shape the body

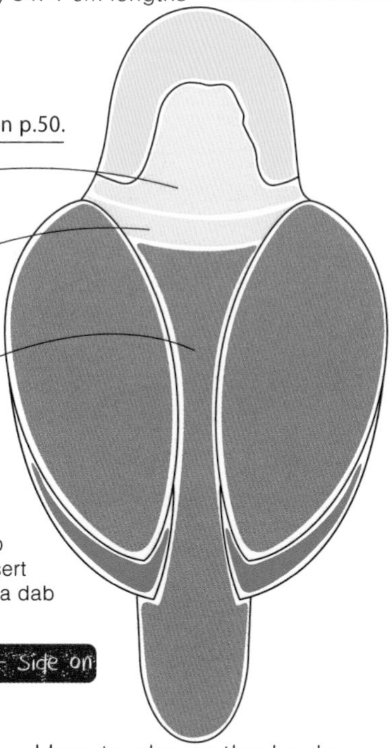

Actual size - Side on

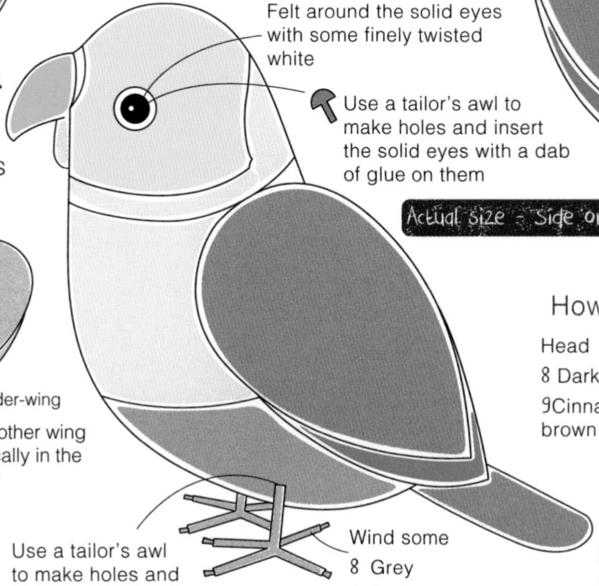

Felt around the solid eyes with some finely twisted white
Use a tailor's awl to make holes and insert the solid eyes with a dab of glue on them
Use a tailor's awl to make holes and insert the legs with a dab of glue on them
Wind some
8 Grey
9 Beige grey
around the wire

How to make the wings

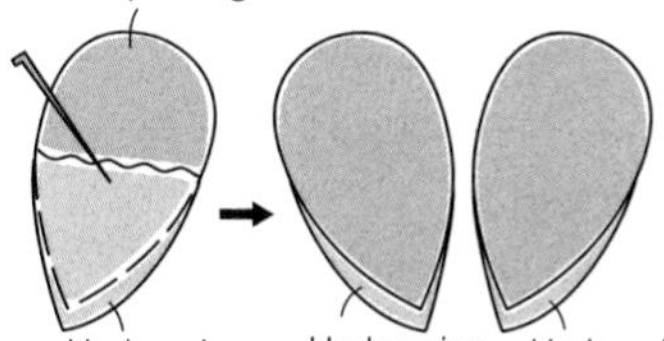

Top-wing reverse
Under-wing
Under-wing
Under-wing
Lay the under-wing onto the top-wing from the reverse side of the top-wing and felt it in place
Make the other wing symmetrically in the same way

How to shape the body

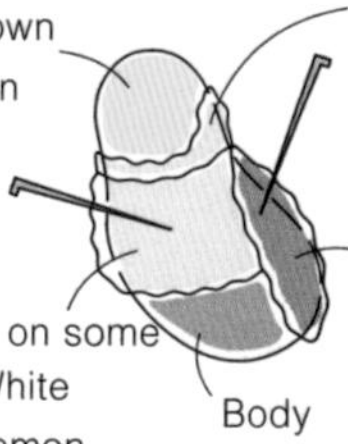

Head
8 Dark brown
9Cinnamon brown
Lay on some
8 Grey
9 Golden yellow
and felt it in
Lay some
8 Cerulean blue
9 Dark green
over the back and felt in
Lay on some
8 White
9 Lemon yellow
and felt it in
Body
8 Aqua
9 Young leaf

8 & 9 Actual-size - components

Head
Lay on 2 g of
8 Dark brown
9 Cinnamon Brown

Body
Lay on 2 g of
8 Aqua
9 Young leaf

Base A x 1

Beak x 1
8 Light pink
9 Vermilion
Thickness 8 mm

Top-wing x 2
8 Cerulean blue
9 Dark green
Thickness 3 mm

Under-wing x 2
8 Grey
9 Navy blue
Thickness 2 mm

Tail feather x 1
8 Cerulean blue
9 Dark green
Tail joint
Leave unfelted
Tekno Rote
Thickness 3 mm

10 & 11 Actual-size - components

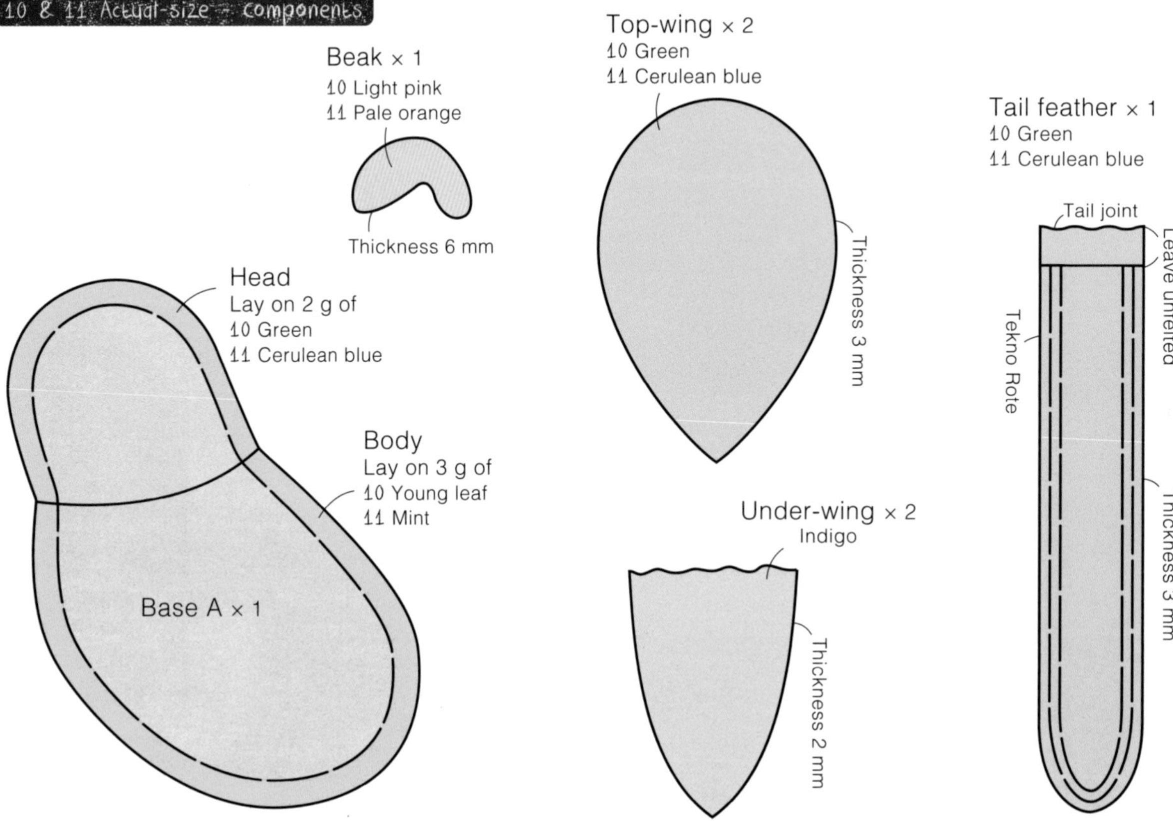
Beak x 1
10 Light pink
11 Pale orange
Thickness 6 mm
Head
Lay on 2 g of
10 Green
11 Cerulean blue
Body
Lay on 3 g of
10 Young leaf
11 Mint
Base A x 1
Top-wing x 2
10 Green
11 Cerulean blue
Thickness 3 mm
Under-wing x 2
Indigo
Thickness 2 mm
Tail feather x 1
10 Green
11 Cerulean blue
Tail joint
Leave unfelted
Tekno Rote
Thickness 3 mm

10 & 11 Monk parakeet

Materials for 10

Felt wool

Solid
- Off-white, 4 g
- Young leaf, 3 g
- Indigo, small amount

Natural Blend
- Green, 4 g
- Grey
- Olive
- Light pink, small amounts

Felting yarn loop
- Light brown, 20 cm

Solid eyes • 4 mm x 2

Other materials
- Clear plastic wallet 2 cm × 13 cm
- Floral wire (brown, 24 gauge) 8 x 3-cm lengths
- Tekno Rote 15 cm
- Floral tape, amount to suit

Materials for 11a

Felt wool

Solid
- Off-white, 4 g
- Indigo
- Grey, small amounts

Natural Blend
- Cerulean blue, 4 g
- Mint, 3 g
- Grey
- Pale orange, small amounts

Felting yarn loop
- Light brown, 20 cm

Solid eyes • 4 mm x 2

Other materials
- Clear plastic wallet 2 cm × 13 cm
- Floral wire (brown, 24 gauge) 8 x 3-cm lengths
- Tekno Rote 15 cm
- Floral tape, amount to suit

Instructions

※For basic instructions to help you make the birds, see pp.34 to 40.

1 Make the base.
2 Felt the wool of the head and body onto the base.
3 Lay the wool indicated in the instructions over the head and body and felt it on.
4 Make and attach the tail feathers.
5 Make and attach the wings.
6 Make and attach the beak.
7 Make the face.
8 Attach the breast feathers.
9 Make and attach the legs.

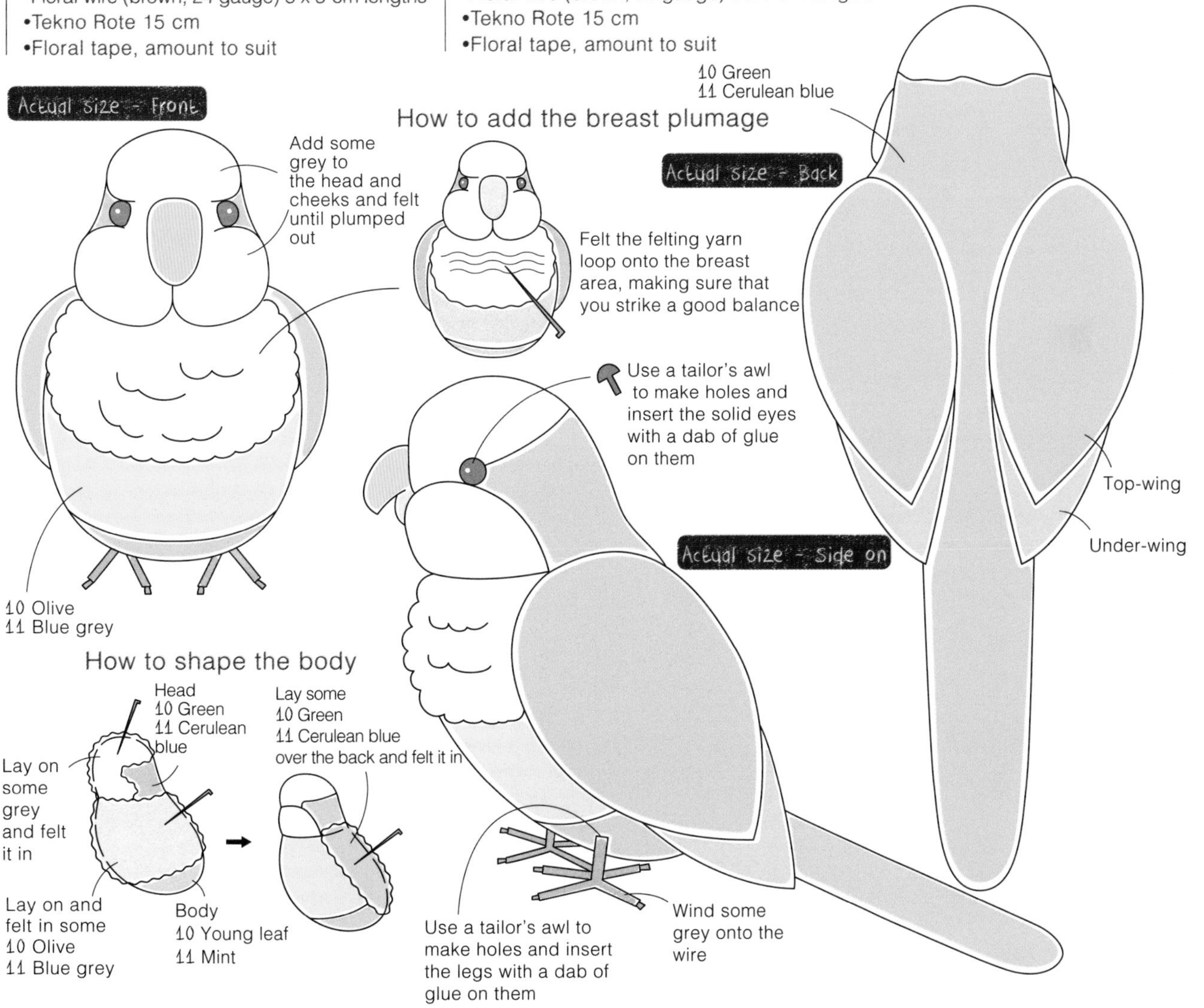

Actual size – Front
Add some grey to the head and cheeks and felt until plumped out
10 Olive
11 Blue grey
How to add the breast plumage
Felt the felting yarn loop onto the breast area, making sure that you strike a good balance
Actual size – Back
10 Green
11 Cerulean blue
Top-wing
Under-wing
Use a tailor's awl to make holes and insert the solid eyes with a dab of glue on them
Actual size – Side on
How to shape the body
Head
10 Green
11 Cerulean blue
Lay on some grey and felt it in
Lay on and felt in some
10 Olive
11 Blue grey
Body
10 Young leaf
11 Mint
Lay some
10 Green
11 Cerulean blue
over the back and felt it in
Use a tailor's awl to make holes and insert the legs with a dab of glue on them
Wind some grey onto the wire

Page 13

12 Bourke's parrot

Materials

Felt wool

Solid
- •Off-white, 4 g
- •Light pink, 6 g
- •White •Lemon yellow
- •Salmon pink, small amounts

Natural Blend
- •Light beige, small amounts

Solid eyes •4 mm x 2

Other materials

- •Clear plastic wallet 2 cm x 13 cm
- •Floral wire (brown, 24 gauge) 8 x 3-cm lengths
- •Tekno Rote 13 cm
- •Floral tape, amount to suit

※The actual-size components are on p.80.

Instructions

※For basic instructions to help you make the birds, see pp.34 to 40.

1 Make the base.
2 Felt the wool of the head and body onto the base.
3 Lay the wool indicated in the instructions over the head and body and felt it on.
4 Make and attach the tail feathers.
5 Make and attach the wings.
6 Make and attach the beak.
7 Make the face.
8 Make and attach the legs.

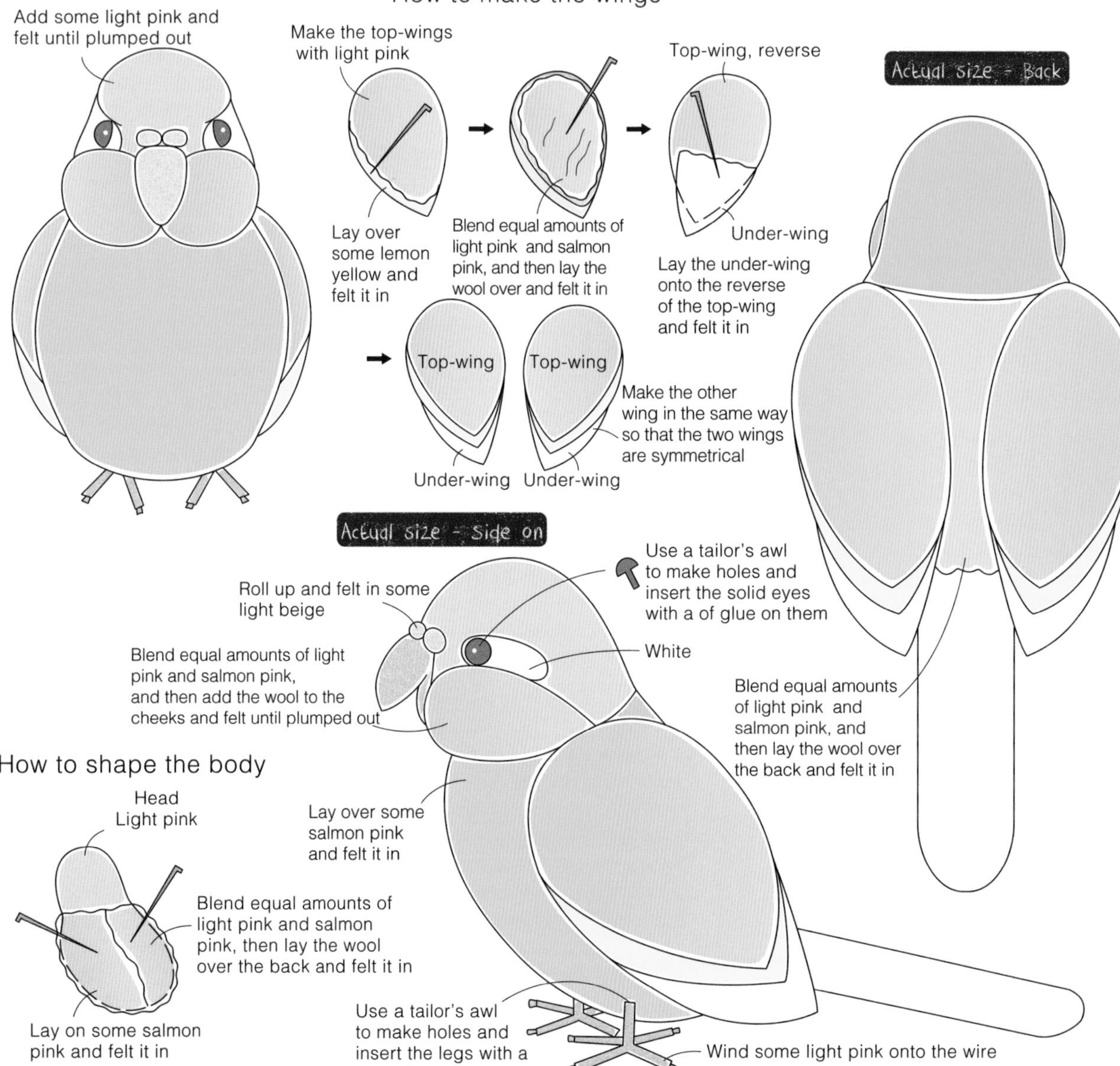

Actual size - Front
Add some light pink and felt until plumped out
How to make the wings
Make the top-wings with light pink
Lay over some lemon yellow and felt it in
Blend equal amounts of light pink and salmon pink, and then lay the wool over and felt it in
Top-wing, reverse
Under-wing
Lay the under-wing onto the reverse of the top-wing and felt it in
Top-wing
Top-wing
Make the other wing in the same way so that the two wings are symmetrical
Under-wing
Under-wing
Actual size - Back
Actual size - Side on
Roll up and felt in some light beige
Use a tailor's awl to make holes and insert the solid eyes with a of glue on them
White
Blend equal amounts of light pink and salmon pink, and then add the wool to the cheeks and felt until plumped out
Blend equal amounts of light pink and salmon pink, and then lay the wool over the back and felt it in
How to shape the body
Head
Light pink
Lay over some salmon pink and felt it in
Blend equal amounts of light pink and salmon pink, then lay the wool over the back and felt it in
Lay on some salmon pink and felt it in
Use a tailor's awl to make holes and insert the legs with a dab of glue on them
Wind some light pink onto the wire

13 White-bellied parrot

Materials

Felt wool

Solid
- •Off-white, 4 g
- •White, 4 g •Golden yellow , 4 g
- •Dark green, 2 g
- •Pale orange, small amount

Natural Blend
- •Light beige
- •Beige grey, small amounts

Felt wool
- •Clear plastic wallet 2 cm x 13 cm
- •Floral wire (brown, 24 gauge) 8 x 4-cm lengths
- •Tekno Rote 37 cm
- •Floral tape, amount to suit

Solid eyes •4 mm x 2

※The actual-size components are on p.80.

Instructions

※For basic instructions to help you make the birds, see pp.34 to 40.

1 Make the base.
2 Felt the wool of the head and body onto the base.
3 Lay the wool indicated in the instructions over the head and body and felt it on.
4 Make the tail feathers and attach them in the order C followed by B and then A.
5 Make and attach the wings.
6 Make and attach the beak.
7 Make the face.
8 Make and attach the legs.

Actual size - Front
Felt around the solid eyes with some finely twisted white
Use a tailor's awl to make the holes, and insert the solid eyes with a dab of glue on them
Add 1 g of white to the breast and felt until plumped out

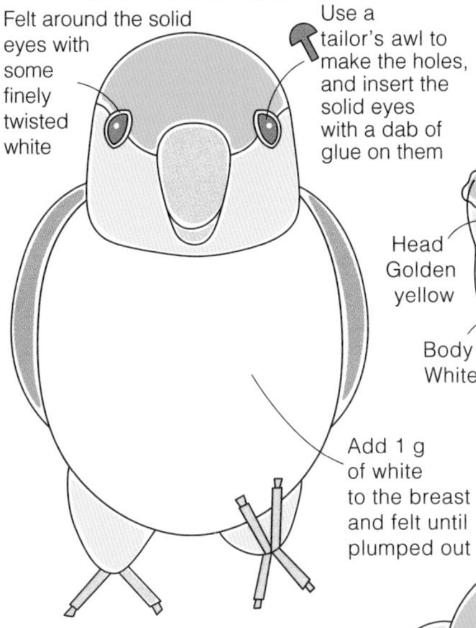

How to shape the body

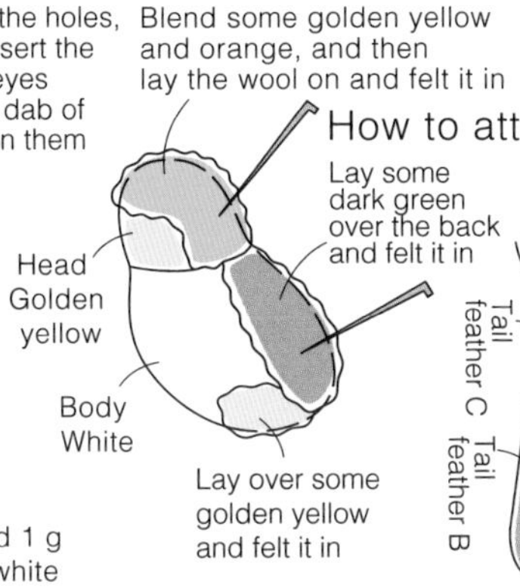

Blend some golden yellow and orange, and then lay the wool on and felt it in
Head Golden yellow
Body White
Lay some dark green over the back and felt it in
Lay over some golden yellow and felt it in

How to attach the tail feathers

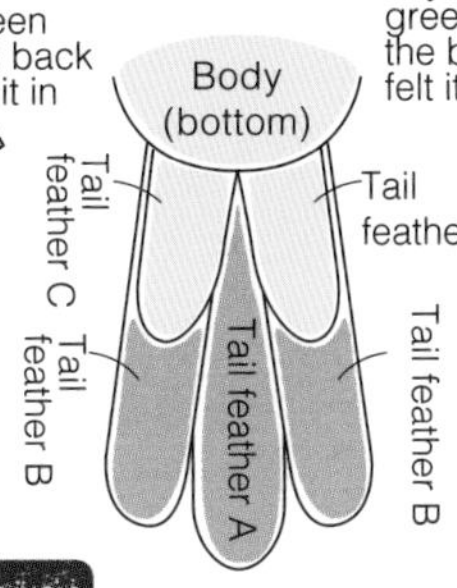

Body (bottom)
Tail feather C
Tail feather C
Tail feather B
Tail feather A
Tail feather B

Actual size - Back
Lay some dark green over the back and felt it in
Tail feather B
Tail feather B
Tail feather A

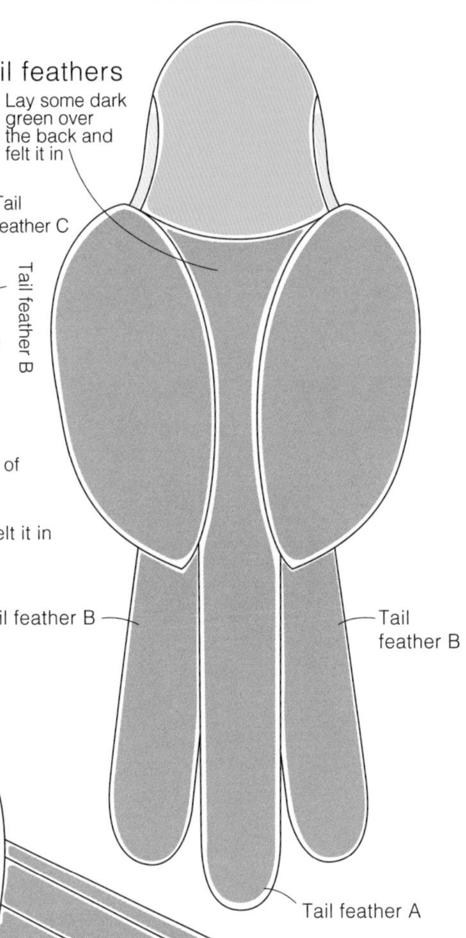

Actual size - Side on
Blend equal amounts of golden yellow and orange, then lay the colour over and felt it in
Golden yellow
Wind some beige-grey onto the wire
Tail feather C

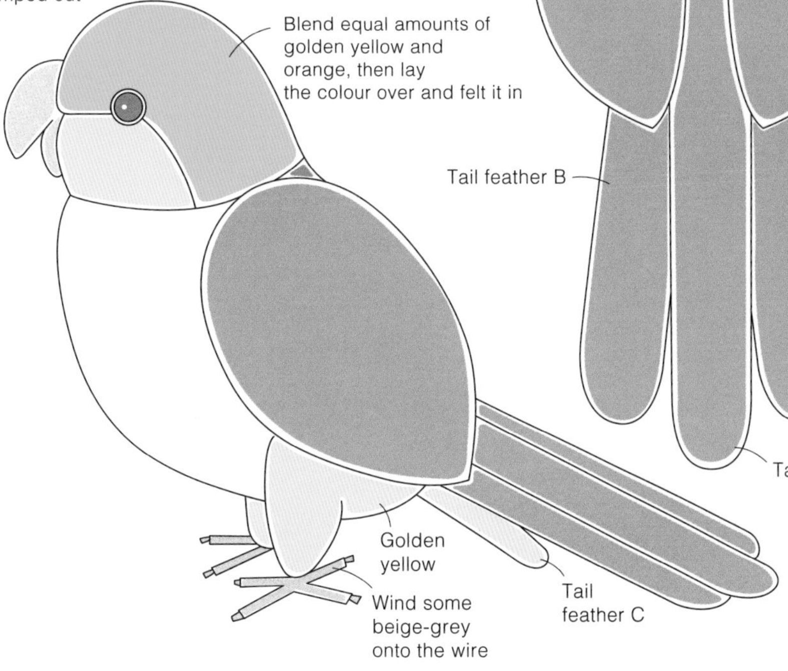

How to attach the legs

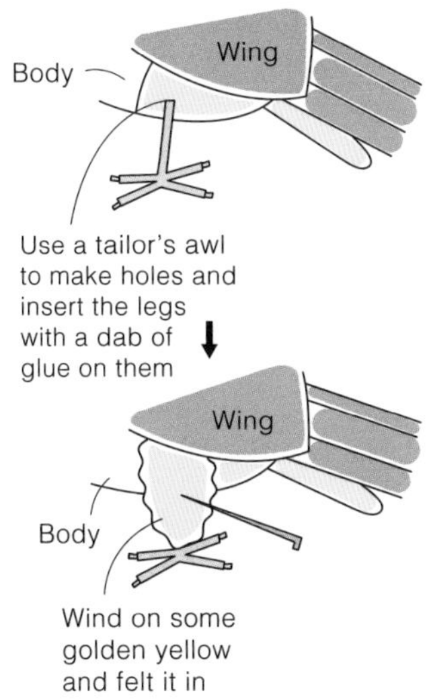

Body
Wing
Use a tailor's awl to make holes and insert the legs with a dab of glue on them
Wing
Body
Wind on some golden yellow and felt it in

Page 15

14 Eastern rosella

Materials

Felt wool

	•Off-white, 4 g
Solid	•White •Young leaf, 3 g of each
	•Violet blue •Dark green, 1 g of each
Natural Blend	
	•Custard, 1 g
	•Light beige •Mint
	•Red •Beige grey, small amounts
Mix	•Black, small amount

Solid eyes •4.5 mm x 2

Other materials

- •Clear plastic wallet 2 cm × 15 cm
- •Floral wire (brown, 24 gauge) 8 x 3-cm lengths
- •Tekno Rote 40 cm
- •Floral tape, amount to suit

Instructions

※For basic instructions to help you make the birds, see pp.34 to 40.

1 Make the base.

2 Felt the wool of the head and body onto the base.

3 Lay the wool indicated in the instructions over the head and body and felt it on.

4 Make and attach the tail feathers.

5 Make and attach the wings.

6 Make and attach the beak.

7 Make the face.

8 Make and attach the legs.

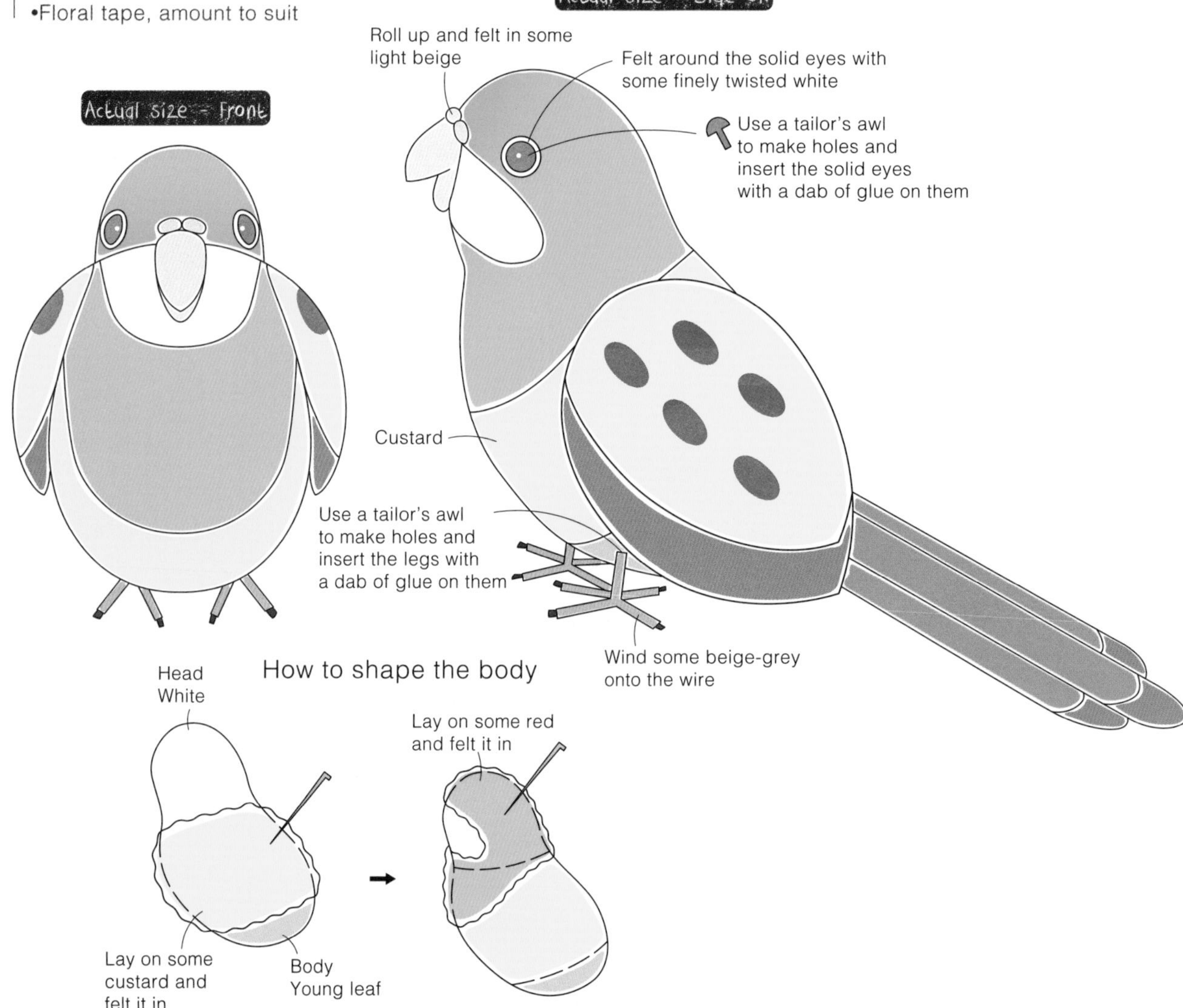
Actual size - Side on
Roll up and felt in some light beige
Felt around the solid eyes with some finely twisted white
Use a tailor's awl to make holes and insert the solid eyes with a dab of glue on them
Actual size - Front
Custard
Use a tailor's awl to make holes and insert the legs with a dab of glue on them
Wind some beige-grey onto the wire
How to shape the body
Head White
Lay on some red and felt it in
Lay on some custard and felt it in
Body Young leaf

Actual size - Back

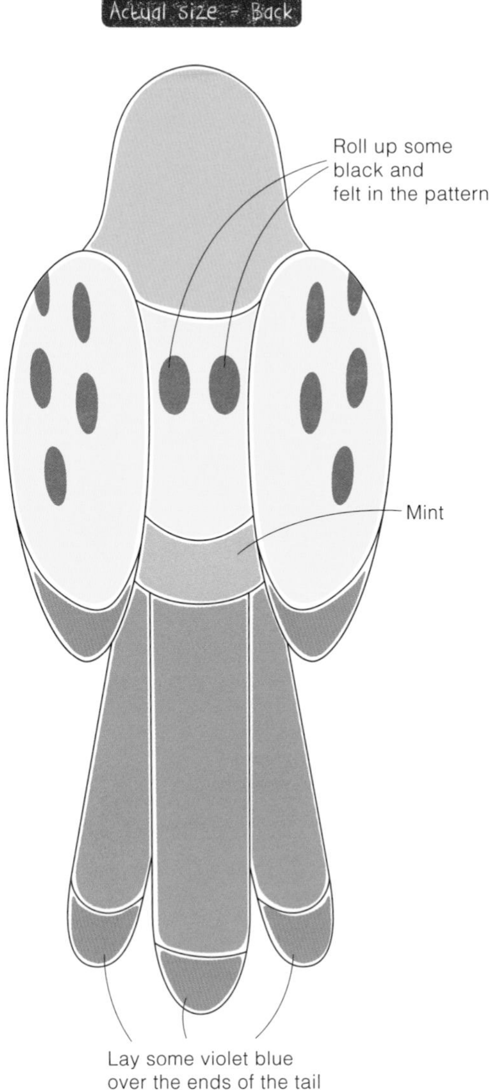

Roll up some black and felt in the pattern
Mint
Lay some violet blue over the ends of the tail feathers and felt it in

How to attach the tail feathers

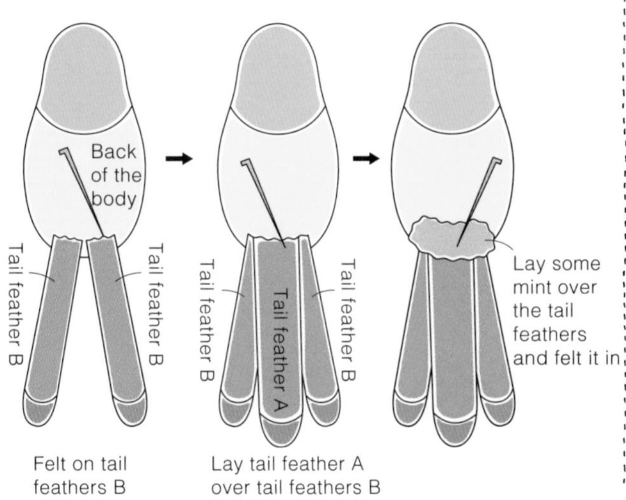

Back of the body
Tail feather B
Tail feather B
Tail feather B
Tail feather A
Tail feather B
Lay some mint over the tail feathers and felt it in
Felt on tail feathers B
Lay tail feather A over tail feathers B and felt it on

Actual size - components

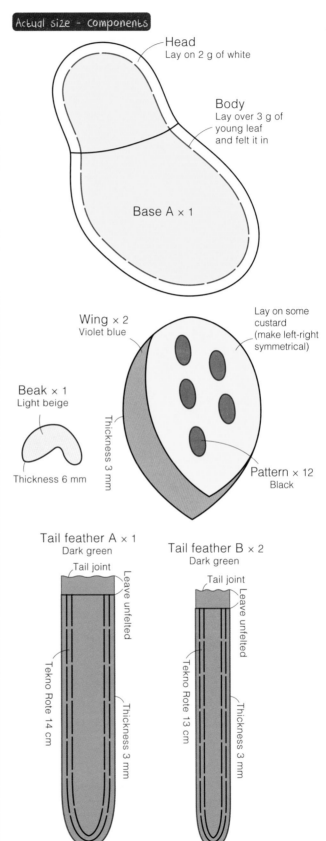

Head
Lay on 2 g of white

Body
Lay over 3 g of young leaf and felt it in

Base A × 1

Wing × 2
Violet blue

Lay on some custard (make left-right symmetrical)

Thickness 3 mm

Pattern × 12
Black

Beak × 1
Light beige

Thickness 6 mm

Tail feather A × 1
Dark green

Tail joint

Leave unfelted

Tekno Rote 14 cm

Thickness 3 mm

Tail feather B × 2
Dark green

Tail joint

Leave unfelted

Tekno Rote 13 cm

Thickness 3 mm

Page 16

15 Scarlet macaw

Materials

Felt wool

- Solid
  - •Off-white, 6 g
  - •Indigo, 2 g
- Natural Blend
  - •Red, 8 g
  - •Pale orange, 1.5 g
  - •Undyed •Light beige
  - •Beige grey, small amounts
- Mix
  - •Black, small amount

Solid eyes •3 mm x 2

Other materials

- •Clear plastic wallet 2 cm × 16 cm
- •Floral wire (brown, 24 gauge) 8 x 4-cm lengths
- •Tekno Rote 76 cm
- •Floral tape, amount to suit

Instructions

※For basic instructions to help you make the birds, see pp.34 to 40.

1 Make the base.

2 Felt the wool of the head and body onto the base.

3 Lay the wool indicated in the instructions over the head and felt it on.

4 Make the tail feathers and attach them in the order C followed by B and then A.

5 Make and attach the wings.

6 Make the upper and lower beaks and attach the lower beak followed by the upper.

7 Make the face

8 Make and attach the legs.

Use a tailor's awl to make holes and insert the solid eyes with a dab of glue on them

Add some red and felt until plumped out

Upper beak

Lower beak

Lay on some undyed and felt it in

Actual size - Side on

Use a needle punch to make holes and insert the legs with a dab of glue on them

Wind some beige-grey onto the wire

Tail feather C

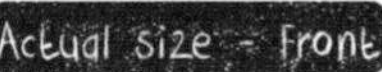
Actual size - Front

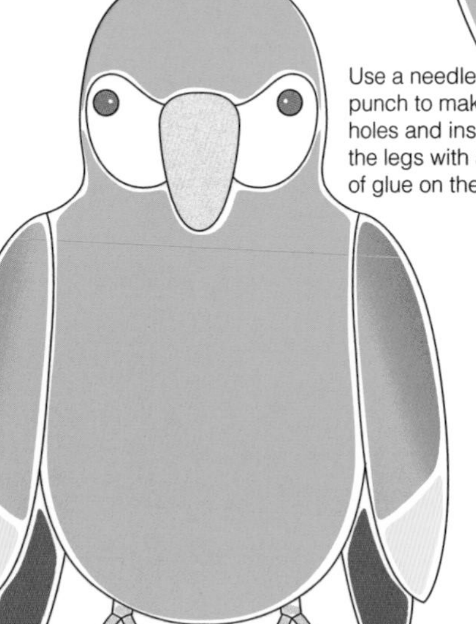

How to attach the tail feathers

Body (Bottom)

Tail feather C

Tail feather C

Tail feather B

Tail feather B

Tail feather A

How to make the wings

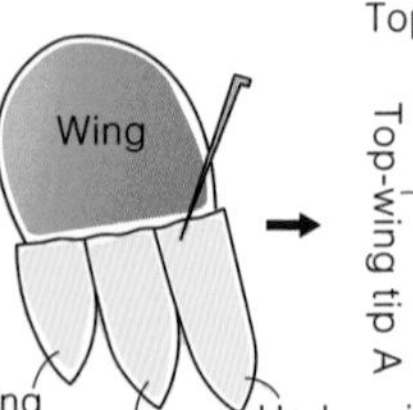
Wing
Under-wing tip A
Under-wing tip B
Under-wing tip C

Lay under-wing tips A, B, and C onto the wing and felt them on

Top-wing tip B

Wing

Top-wing tip A

Top-wing tip C

Felt on top wing tips A, B, and C

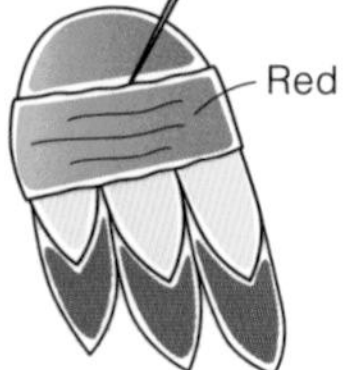
Red

Lay some red over the top-wing tips and felt it on

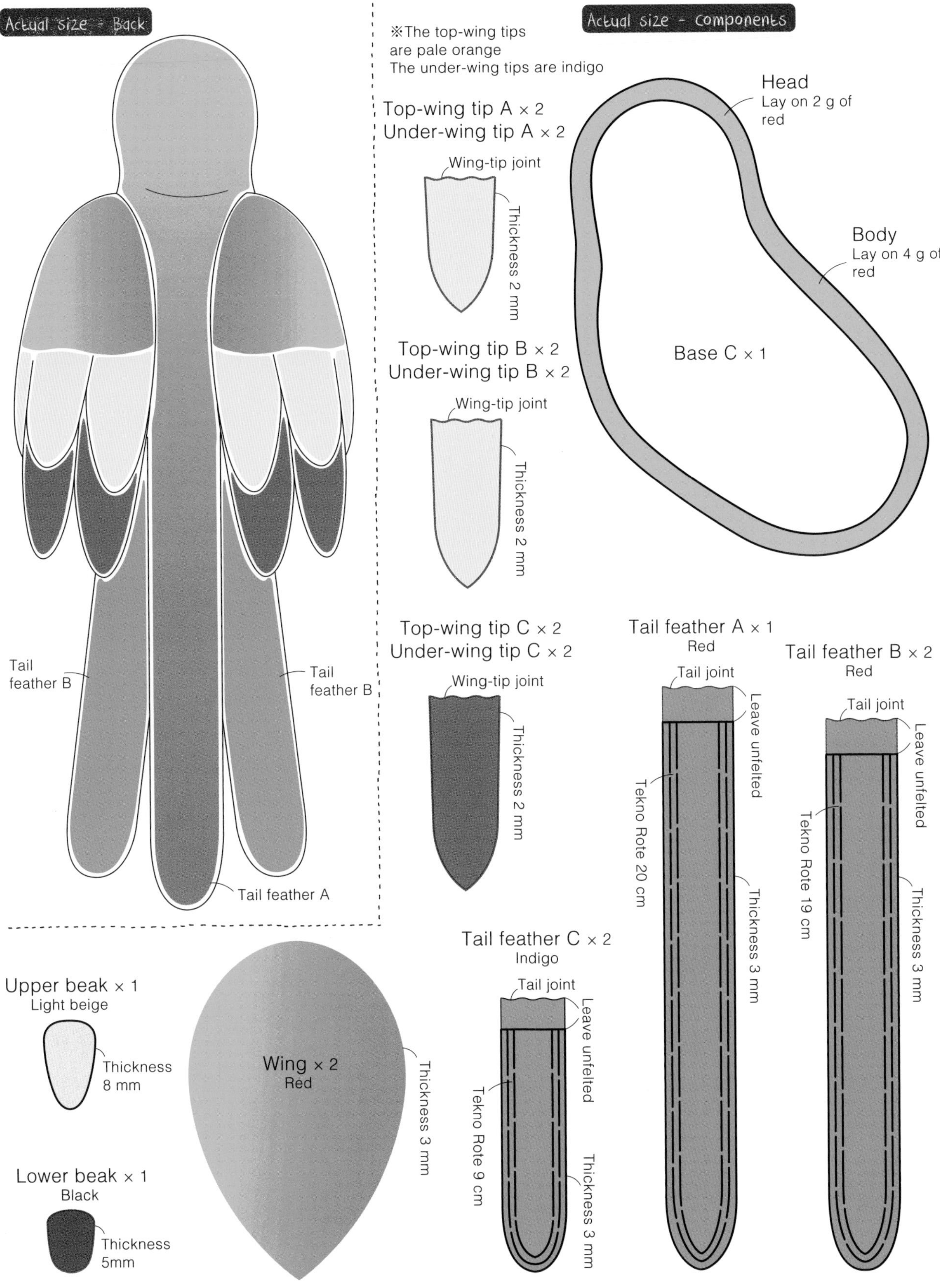

Actual size - Back
Tail feather B
Tail feather B
Tail feather A
※The top-wing tips are pale orange
The under-wing tips are indigo
Top-wing tip A × 2
Under-wing tip A × 2
Wing-tip joint
Thickness 2 mm
Top-wing tip B × 2
Under-wing tip B × 2
Wing-tip joint
Thickness 2 mm
Top-wing tip C × 2
Under-wing tip C × 2
Wing-tip joint
Thickness 2 mm
Actual size - components
Head
Lay on 2 g of red
Body
Lay on 4 g of red
Base C × 1
Tail feather A × 1
Red
Tail joint
Leave unfelted
Tekno Rote 20 cm
Thickness 3 mm
Tail feather B × 2
Red
Tail joint
Leave unfelted
Tekno Rote 19 cm
Thickness 3 mm
Upper beak × 1
Light beige
Thickness 8 mm
Lower beak × 1
Black
Thickness 5mm
Wing × 2
Red
Thickness 3 mm
Tail feather C × 2
Indigo
Tail joint
Leave unfelted
Tekno Rote 9 cm
Thickness 3 mm

Page 17 **16 Blue-and-yellow macaw**

Materials

Felt wool

Solid	•Off-white, 6 g •Indigo, 3 g •Young grass • Dark green, small amounts
Natural Blend	•Pale orange, 5 g •Cerulean blue, 4 g •Undyed •Beige grey, small amounts
Mix	•Black, 1 g

Solid eyes •3 mm x 2

Other materials

- •Clear plastic wallet 2 cm x 16 cm
- •Floral wire (brown, 24 gauge) 8 x 4-cm lengths
- •Tekno Rote 76 cm
- •Floral tape, amount to suit

Instructions

※For basic instructions to help you make the birds, see pp.34 to 40.

1 Make the base.
2 Felt the wool of the head and body onto the base.
3 Lay the wool indicated in the instructions over the head and body and then felt it on.
(Felt the wool on by following steps ① to ⑦ shown around the illustration below)
4 Make the tail feathers and attach them in the order C followed by B and then A.
5 Make and attach the wings.
6 Make and attach the beak.
7 Attach the eyes.
8 Make and attach the legs.

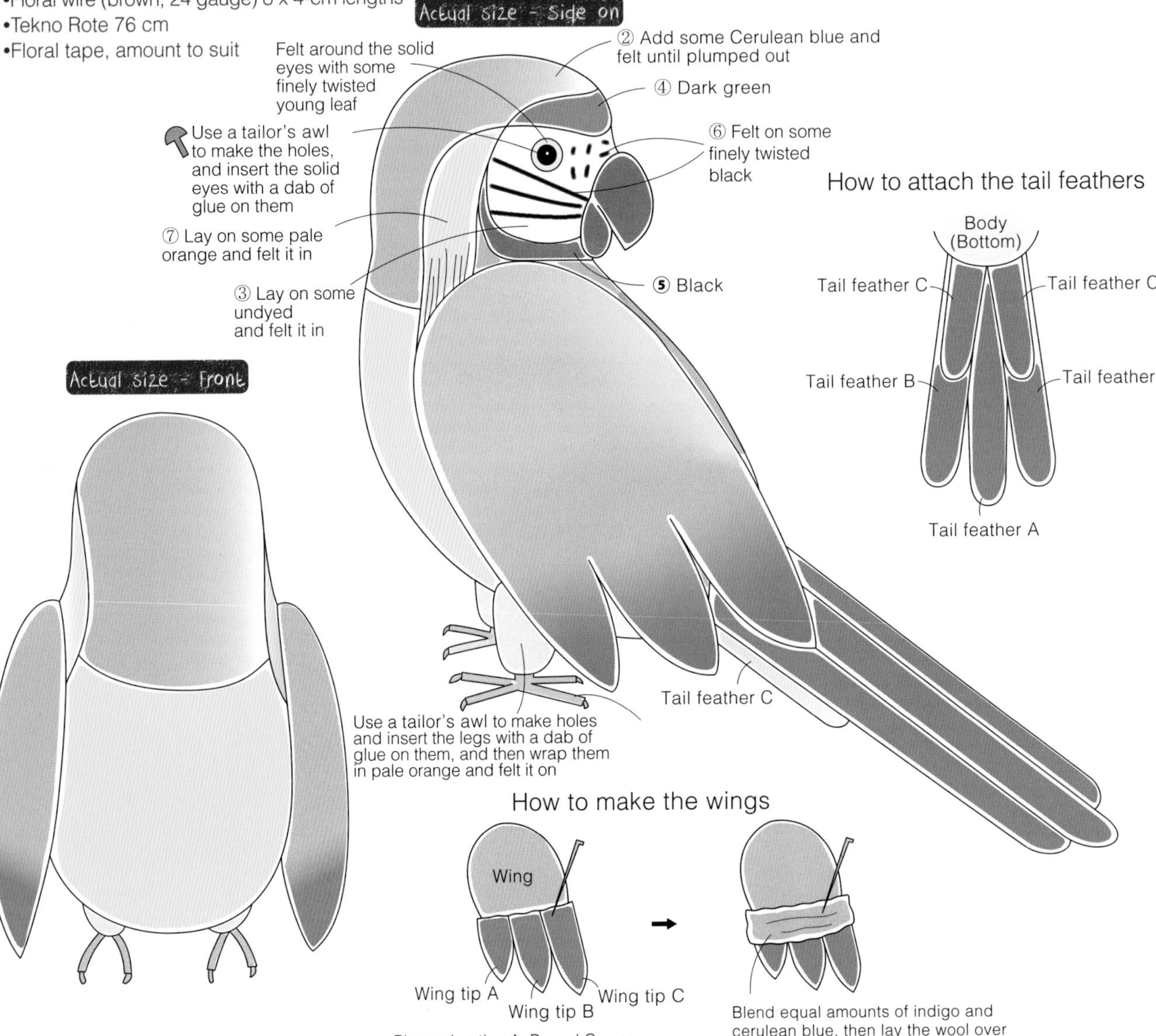

Actual size - Side on
② Add some Cerulean blue and felt until plumped out
Felt around the solid eyes with some finely twisted young leaf
④ Dark green
Use a tailor's awl to make the holes, and insert the solid eyes with a dab of glue on them
⑥ Felt on some finely twisted black
⑦ Lay on some pale orange and felt it in
③ Lay on some undyed and felt it in
⑤ Black
Actual size - Front
Tail feather C
Use a tailor's awl to make holes and insert the legs with a dab of glue on them, and then wrap them in pale orange and felt it on
How to attach the tail feathers
Body (Bottom)
Tail feather C
Tail feather C
Tail feather B
Tail feather B
Tail feather A
How to make the wings
Wing
Wing tip A
Wing tip B
Wing tip C
Place wing tips A, B, and C over the wing and needle-felt them on
Blend equal amounts of indigo and cerulean blue, then lay the wool over the wing tips and felt it in

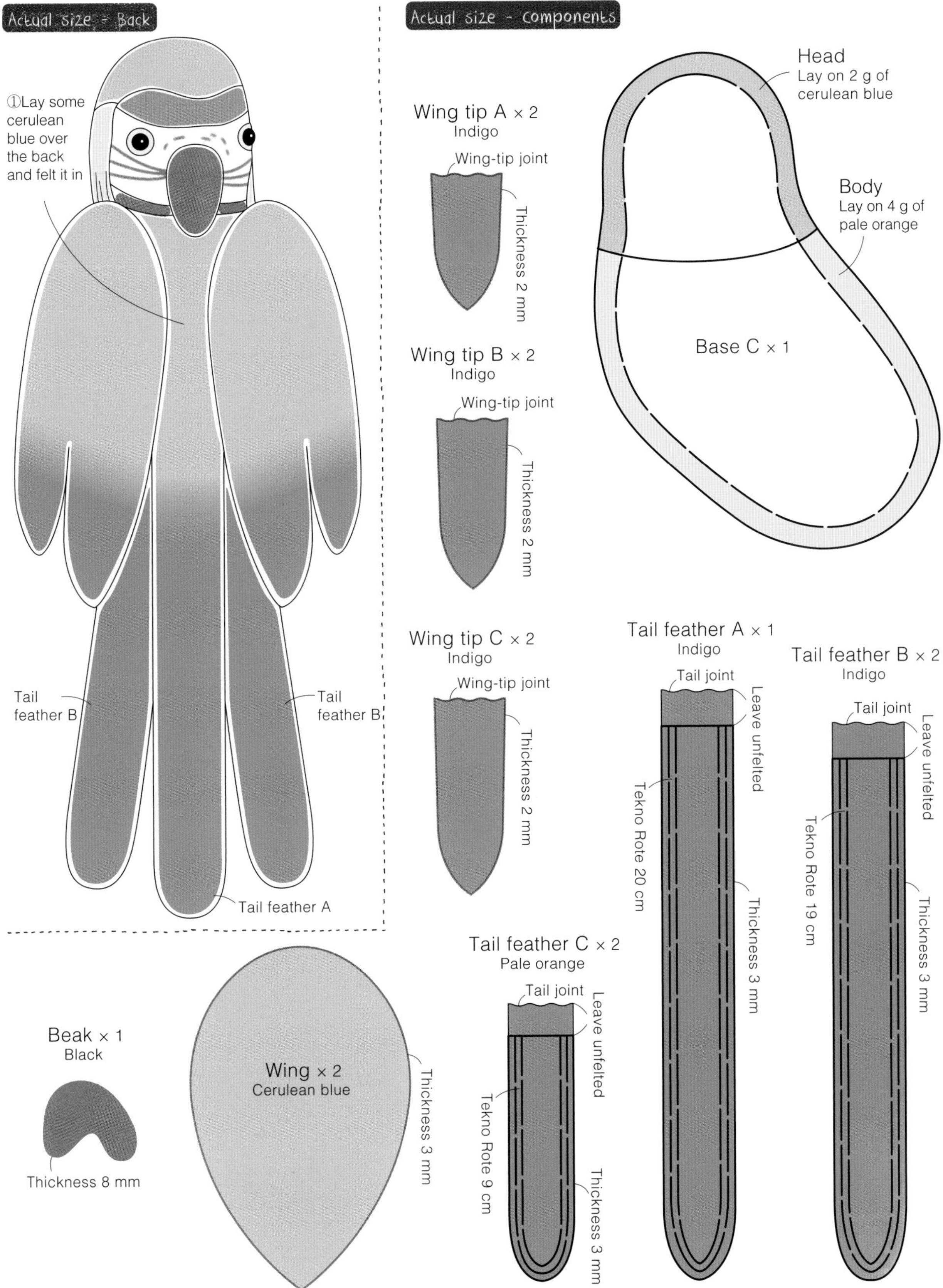
Actual size – Back
①Lay some cerulean blue over the back and felt it in
Tail feather B
Tail feather B
Tail feather A
Actual size – components
Head
Lay on 2 g of cerulean blue
Body
Lay on 4 g of pale orange
Base C × 1
Wing tip A × 2
Indigo
Wing-tip joint
Thickness 2 mm
Wing tip B × 2
Indigo
Wing-tip joint
Thickness 2 mm
Wing tip C × 2
Indigo
Wing-tip joint
Thickness 2 mm
Tail feather A × 1
Indigo
Tail joint
Leave unfelted
Tekno Rote 20 cm
Thickness 3 mm
Tail feather B × 2
Indigo
Tail joint
Leave unfelted
Tekno Rote 19 cm
Thickness 3 mm
Tail feather C × 2
Pale orange
Tail joint
Leave unfelted
Tekno Rote 9 cm
Thickness 3 mm
Beak × 1
Black
Thickness 8 mm
Wing × 2
Cerulean blue
Thickness 3 mm

17 & 18 Sulphur-crested cockatoo

Materials (for one bird)

Felt wool

Solid
- •Off-white, 6 g
- •Aqua (18 only), small amount

Natural Blend
- •Undyed 801, 9 g
- • Grey (17 only) •Dark grey
- •Pale orange, small amounts

Mix
- •Black, small amount

Solid eyes •4 mm x 2

Other materials

- •Clear plastic wallet 2 cm × 15 cm
- •Floral wire (brown, 24 gauge) 8 x 4-cm lengths
- •Tekno Rote 76 cm
- •Floral tape, amount to suit

Instructions

※For basic instructions to help you make the birds, see pp.34 to 40.

1 Make the base.

2 Felt the wool of the head and body onto the base.

3 Lay the wool indicated in the instructions over the head and felt it on.

4 Make and attach the tail feathers.

5 Make and attach the wings.

6 Make and attach the crest.

7 Make and attach the beak.

8 Make the face.

9 Make and attach the legs.

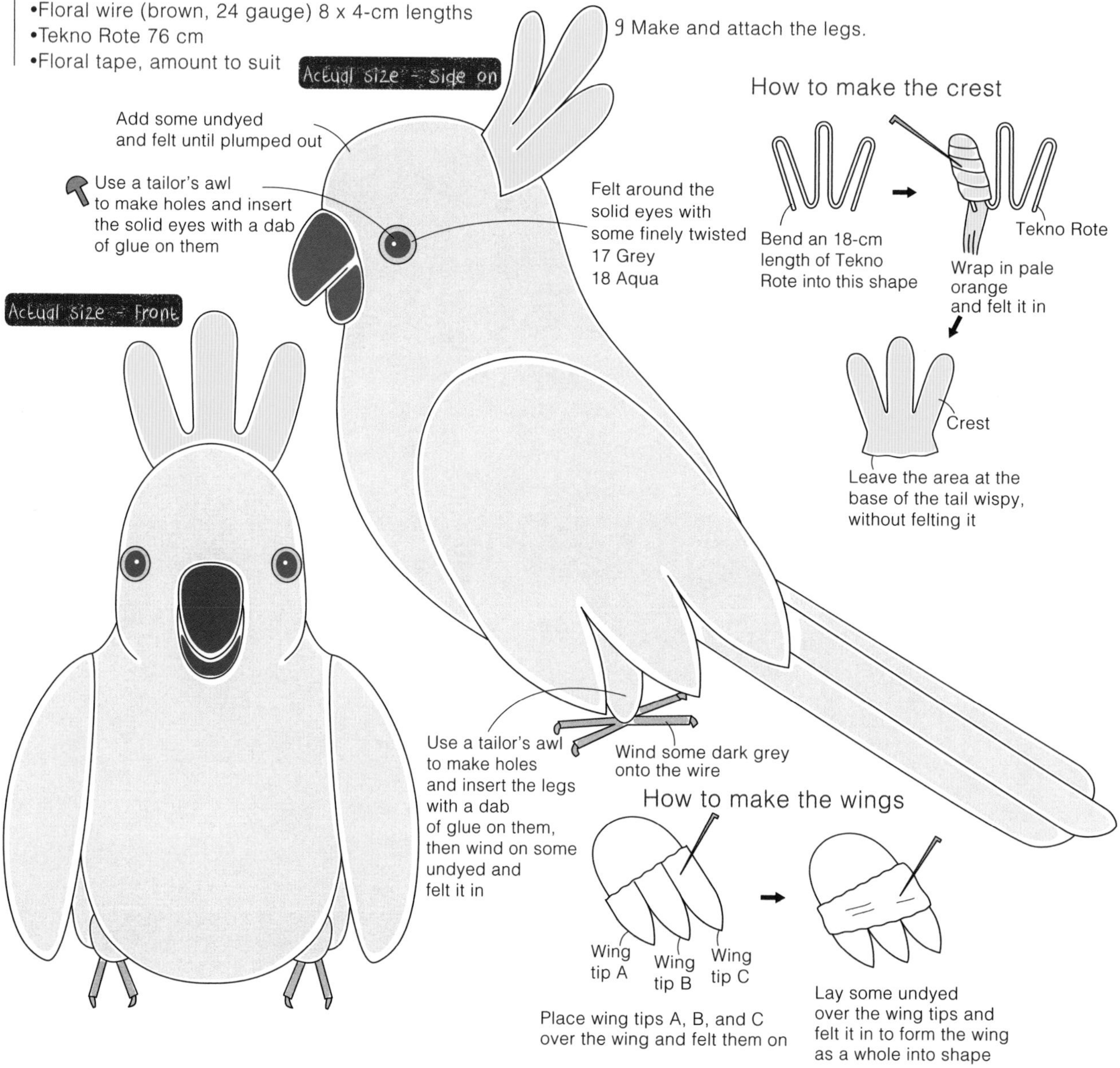

Actual size – Side on

Add some undyed and felt until plumped out

Use a tailor's awl to make holes and insert the solid eyes with a dab of glue on them

Felt around the solid eyes with some finely twisted
17 Grey
18 Aqua

Use a tailor's awl to make holes and insert the legs with a dab of glue on them, then wind on some undyed and felt it in

Wind some dark grey onto the wire

Actual size – Front

How to make the crest

Bend an 18-cm length of Tekno Rote into this shape

Tekno Rote

Wrap in pale orange and felt it in

Crest

Leave the area at the base of the tail wispy, without felting it

How to make the wings

Wing tip A

Wing tip B

Wing tip C

Place wing tips A, B, and C over the wing and felt them on

Lay some undyed over the wing tips and felt it in to form the wing as a whole into shape

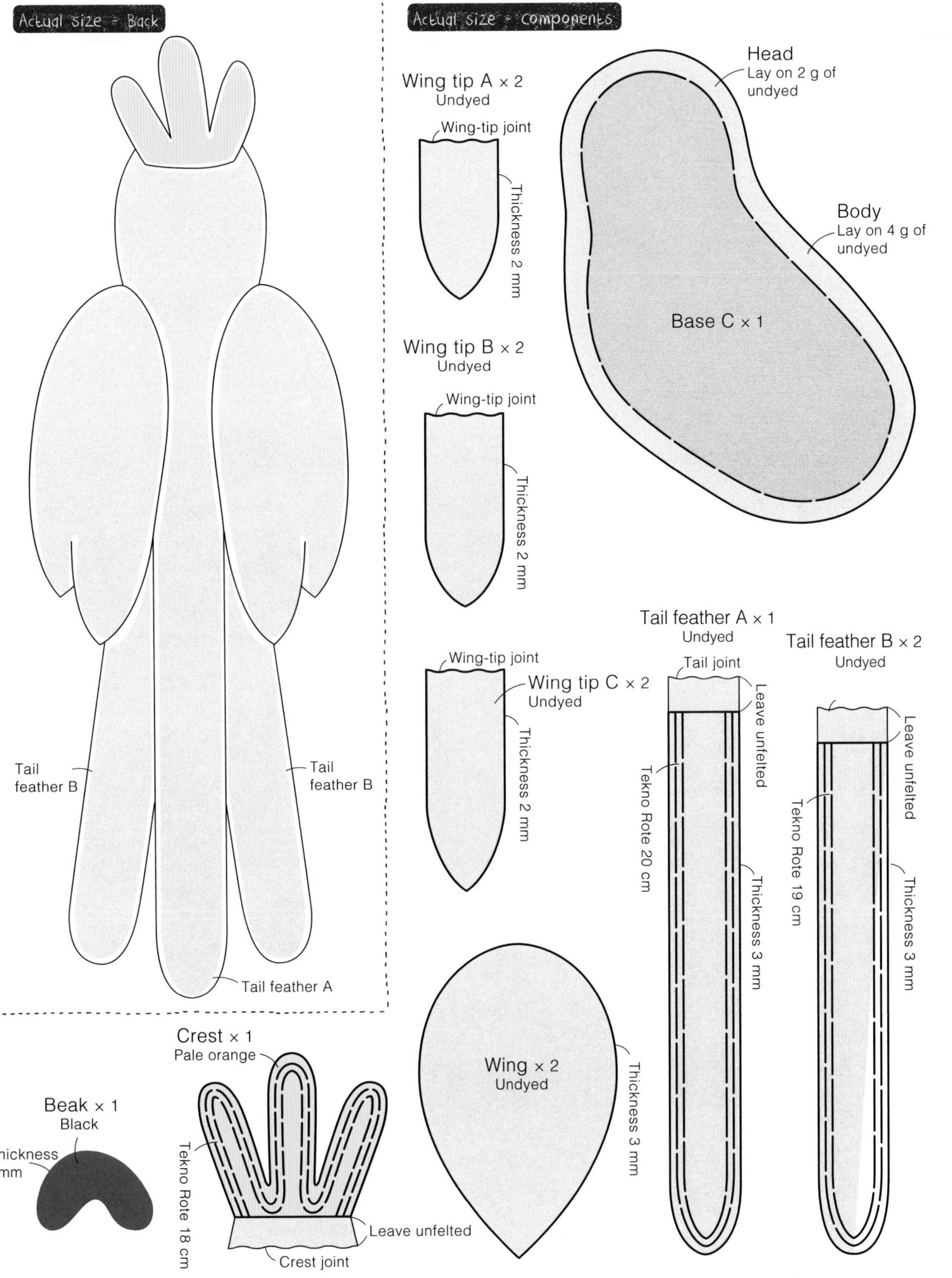
Actual size = Back
Tail feather B
Tail feather B
Tail feather A
Actual size = Components
Wing tip A × 2
Undyed
Wing-tip joint
Thickness 2 mm
Head
Lay on 2 g of undyed
Body
Lay on 4 g of undyed
Base C × 1
Wing tip B × 2
Undyed
Wing-tip joint
Thickness 2 mm
Wing-tip joint
Wing tip C × 2
Undyed
Thickness 2 mm
Tail feather A × 1
Undyed
Tail joint
Leave unfelted
Tekno Rote 20 cm
Thickness 3 mm
Tail feather B × 2
Undyed
Leave unfelted
Tekno Rote 19 cm
Thickness 3 mm
Crest × 1
Pale orange
Tekno Rote 18 cm
Leave unfelted
Crest joint
Beak × 1
Black
Thickness 8mm
Wing × 2
Undyed
Thickness 3 mm

Page 19

19 Toco toucan

Materials

Felt wool

Solid
- •Off-white, 6 g
- •Black, 8 g
- •Orange •Indigo (39), small amounts

Natural Blend
- •Pale orange, 2 g
- •Undyed •Red •Beige grey, small amounts

Solid eyes •4 mm x 2

Other materials

- •Clear plastic wallet 2 cm x 15 cm
- •Floral wire (brown, 24 gauge) 8 x 4-cm lengths
- •Tekno Rote 52 cm
- •Floral tape, amount to suit

Instructions

※For basic instructions to help you make the birds, see pp.34 to 40.

1 Make the base.

2 Felt the wool of the head and body onto the base.

3 Lay the wool indicated in the instructions over the head and body and felt it on.

4 Make and attach the tail feathers.

5 Make and attach the wings.

6 Make and attach the beak.

7 Make the face (following steps ① to ③ shown in the illustration below)

8 Make and attach the legs.

Actual size - Side on

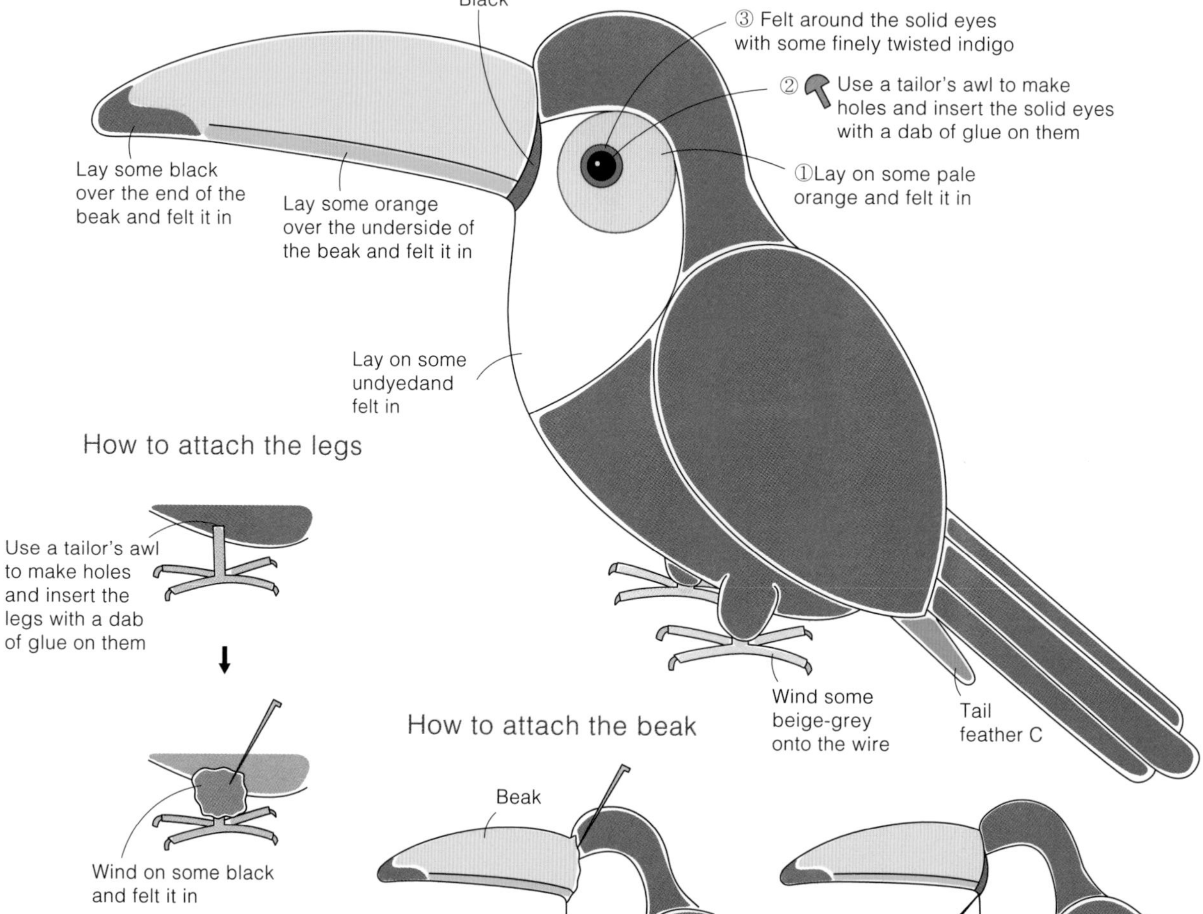

Black
③ Felt around the solid eyes with some finely twisted indigo
② Use a tailor's awl to make holes and insert the solid eyes with a dab of glue on them
①Lay on some pale orange and felt it in
Lay some black over the end of the beak and felt it in
Lay some orange over the underside of the beak and felt it in
Lay on some undyedand felt in
Wind some beige-grey onto the wire
Tail feather C

How to attach the legs

Use a tailor's awl to make holes and insert the legs with a dab of glue on them
Wind on some black and felt it in

How to attach the beak

Beak

Felt the beak firmly onto the head

Felt on some finely twisted black (9) under the beak

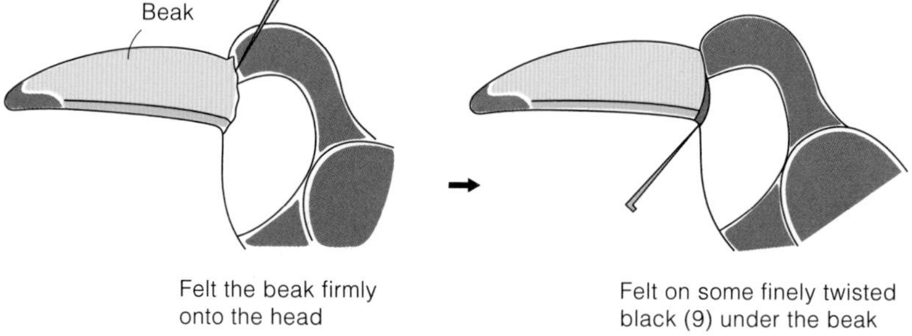

Actual size - Back

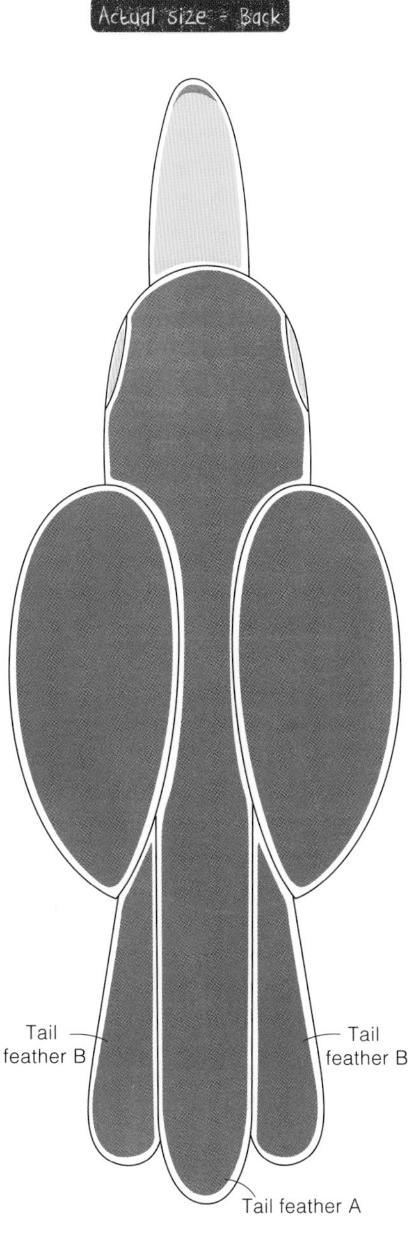
Tail feather B
Tail feather B
Tail feather A

How to attach the tail feathers

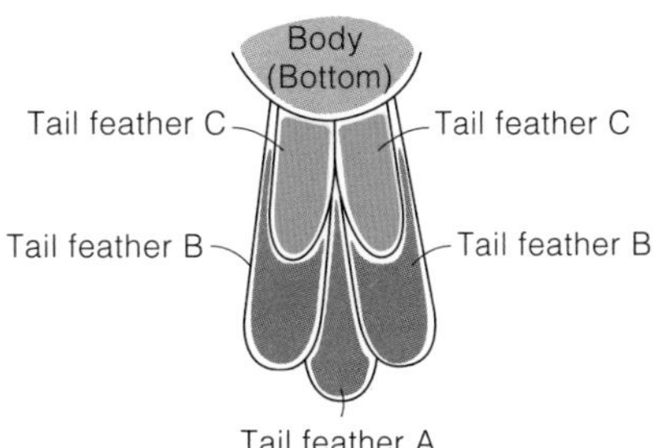
Body (Bottom)
Tail feather C
Tail feather C
Tail feather B
Tail feather B
Tail feather A

Actual size - Components

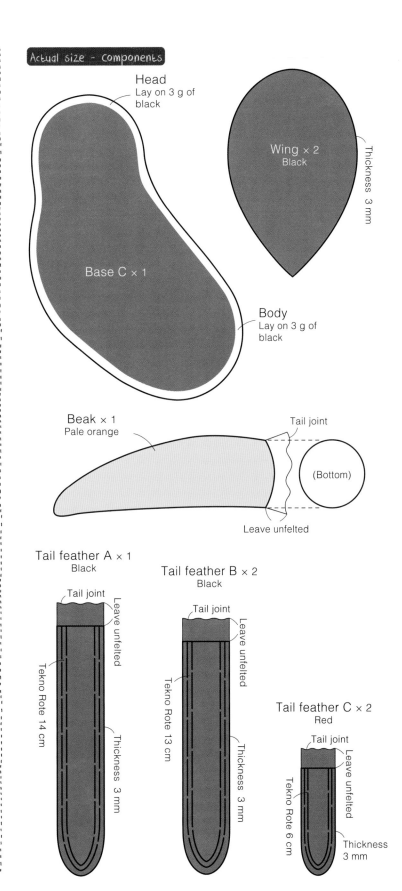

Head
Lay on 3 g of black

Wing × 2
Black
Thickness 3 mm

Base C × 1

Body
Lay on 3 g of black

Beak × 1
Pale orange
Tail joint
(Bottom)
Leave unfelted

Tail feather A × 1
Black
Tail joint
Leave unfelted
Tekno Rote 14 cm
Thickness 3 mm

Tail feather B × 2
Black
Tail joint
Leave unfelted
Tekno Rote 13 cm
Thickness 3 mm

Tail feather C × 2
Red
Tail joint
Leave unfelted
Tekno Rote 6 cm
Thickness 3 mm

Page 20

20 & 21 Java sparrow

Materials for 20

Felt wool

Solid
- Off-white, 4 g
- Madder red
- Light pink), small amounts

Natural Blend
- Undyed, 6 g

Solid eyes •4 mm x 2

Other materials
- Clear plastic wallet 2 cm × 12 cm
- Floral wire (brown, 24 gauge) 8 x 5-cm lengths
- Tekno Rote 10 cm
- Floral tape, amount to suit

Materials for 21

Felt wool

Solid
- Off-white, 4 g
- Black, 3 g
- Madder red
- Light pink, small amounts

Natural Blend
- Grey, 3 g
- Undyed, small amount

Solid eyes •4 mm x 2

Other materials
- Clear plastic wallet 2 cm × 12 cm
- Floral wire (brown, 24 gauge) 8 x 5-cm lengths
- Tekno Rote 10 cm
- Floral tape, amount to suit

Instructions

※For basic instructions to help you make the birds, see pp.34 to 40.

1 Make the base.

2 Felt the wool of the head and body onto the base.

3 Lay the wool indicated in the instructions over the head and body and felt it on (21 only).

4 Make and attach the tail feather.

5 Make and attach the wings.

6 Make and attach the beak.

7 Make the face.

8 Make and attach the legs.

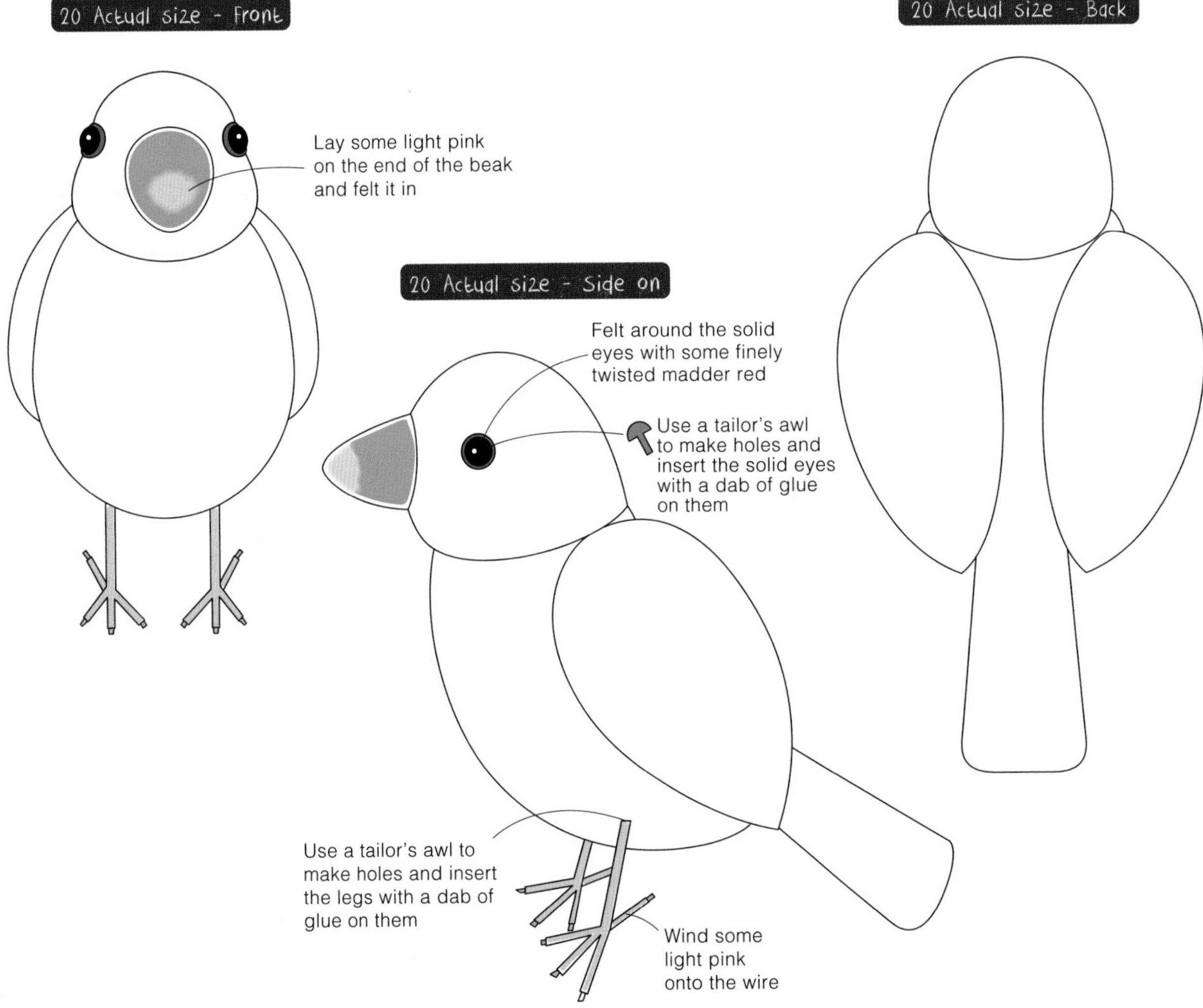
20 Actual size - Front
Lay some light pink on the end of the beak and felt it in
20 Actual size - Back
20 Actual size - Side on
Felt around the solid eyes with some finely twisted madder red
Use a tailor's awl to make holes and insert the solid eyes with a dab of glue on them
Use a tailor's awl to make holes and insert the legs with a dab of glue on them
Wind some light pink onto the wire

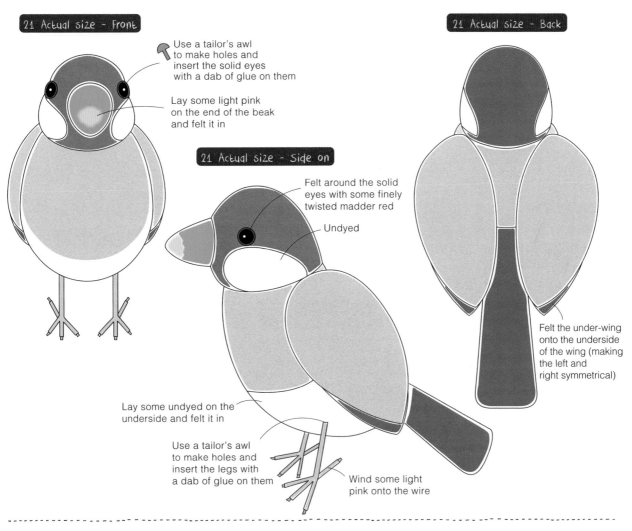

21 Actual size - Front

Use a tailor's awl to make holes and insert the solid eyes with a dab of glue on them

Lay some light pink on the end of the beak and felt it in

21 Actual size - Back

Felt the under-wing onto the underside of the wing (making the left and right symmetrical)

21 Actual size - Side on

Felt around the solid eyes with some finely twisted madder red

Undyed

Lay some undyed on the underside and felt it in

Use a tailor's awl to make holes and insert the legs with a dab of glue on them

Wind some light pink onto the wire

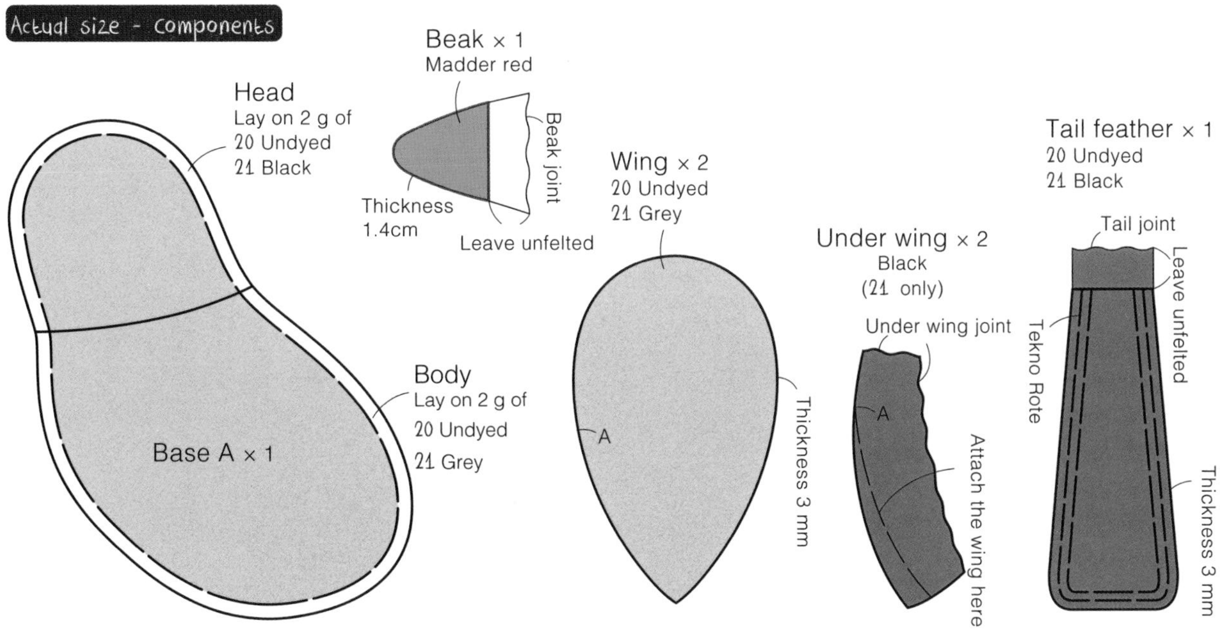

Actual size - components
Beak × 1
Madder red
Beak joint
Thickness 1.4cm
Leave unfelted
Head
Lay on 2 g of
20 Undyed
21 Black
Body
Lay on 2 g of
20 Undyed
21 Grey
Base A × 1
Wing × 2
20 Undyed
21 Grey
A
Thickness 3 mm
Under wing × 2
Black
(21 only)
Under wing joint
A
Attach the wing here
Tail feather × 1
20 Undyed
21 Black
Tail joint
Leave unfelted
Tekno Rote
Thickness 3 mm

Page 23

22 Red-flanked bluetail

Materials

Felt wool

Solid	•Off-white, 3 g •Indigo, 4 g •Black, small amount
Natural Blend	•Undyed, 2 g
Mix	•Pale orange, small amount •Brown •Navy blue, small amounts

Solid eyes •3 mm x 2

Other materials

- •Clear plastic wallet 2 cm × 11 cm
- •Floral wire (brown, 24 gauge) 8 x 4-cm lengths
- •Tekno Rote 9 cm
- •Floral tape, amount to suit

Instructions

※For basic instructions to help you make the birds, see pp.34 to 40.

1 Make the base.
2 Felt the wool of the head and body onto the base.
3 Make and attach the tail feather.
4 Make and attach the wings.
5 Make and attach the beak.
6 Make the face.
7 Make and attach the legs.

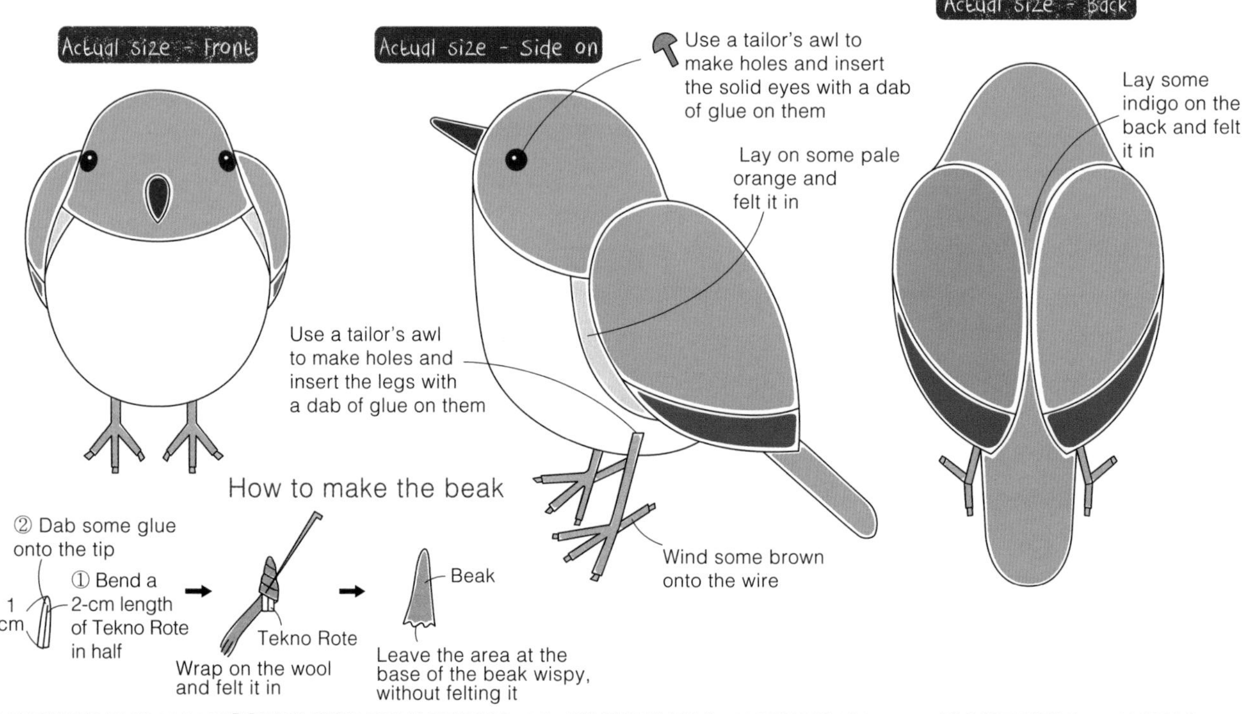
Actual size - Front
Actual size - Side on
Actual size - Back
Use a tailor's awl to make holes and insert the solid eyes with a dab of glue on them
Lay on some pale orange and felt it in
Lay some indigo on the back and felt it in
Use a tailor's awl to make holes and insert the legs with a dab of glue on them
Wind some brown onto the wire
How to make the beak
② Dab some glue onto the tip
① Bend a 2-cm length of Tekno Rote in half
1 cm
Tekno Rote
Wrap on the wool and felt it in
Beak
Leave the area at the base of the beak wispy, without felting it

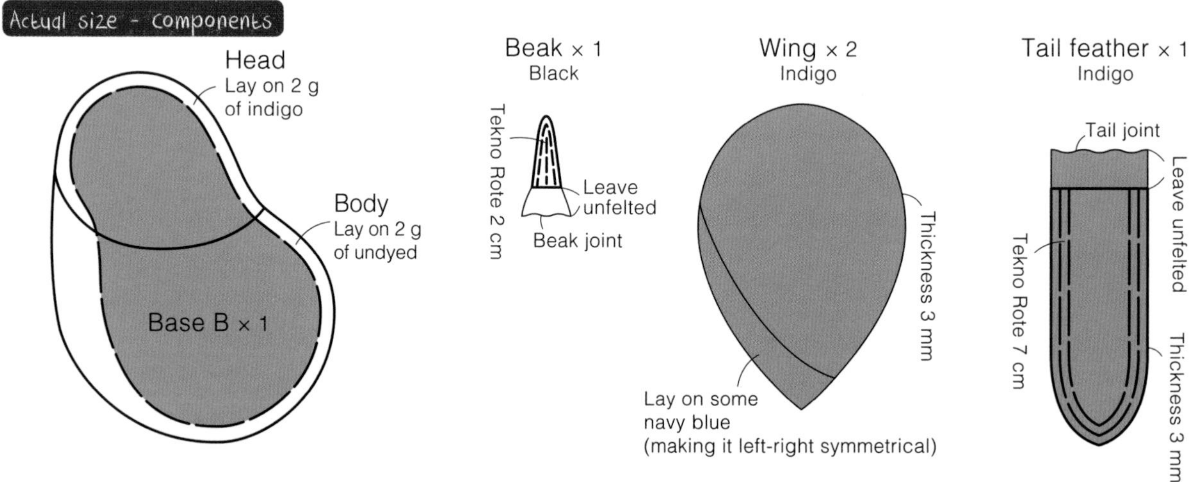
Actual size - components
Head
Lay on 2 g of indigo
Body
Lay on 2 g of undyed
Base B × 1
Beak × 1
Black
Tekno Rote 2 cm
Leave unfelted
Beak joint
Wing × 2
Indigo
Thickness 3 mm
Lay on some navy blue (making it left-right symmetrical)
Tail feather × 1
Indigo
Tail joint
Leave unfelted
Tekno Rote 7 cm
Thickness 3 mm

Page 23

23 Warbling white-eye

Materials

Felt wool

- Solid
  - •Off-white, 3 g
  - •Moss green, 4 g
  - •Black
  - •Dark yellow-green, small amounts
- Natural Blend
  - •Undyed, 2.5 g
  - •Green, small amount
- Mix
  - •Brown, small amount

Solid eyes •3 mm x 2

Other materials

- •Clear plastic wallet 2 cm × 11 cm
- •Floral wire (brown, 24 gauge) 8 x 4-cm lengths
- •Tekno Rote 8 cm
- •Floral tape, amount to suit

Instructions

※For basic instructions to help you make the birds, see pp.34 to 40. For the beak, see p.66.

1 Make the base.

2 Felt the wool of the head and body onto the base.

3 Lay the wool indicated in the instructions over the body and felt it on.

4 Make and attach the tail feather.

5 Make and attach the wings.

6 Make and attach the beak.

7 Make the face.

8 Make and attach the legs.

Actual size - Front

Lay over some dark yellow-green and felt it in

Actual size - Side on

Felt around the solid eyes with some finely twisted undyed

Use a tailor's awl to make holes and insert the solid eyes with a dab of glue on them

Lay on some green and felt it in

Lay some brown over the back and felt it in

Use a tailor's awl to make holes and insert the legs with a dab of glue on them

Wind some brown onto the wire

Actual size - Back

Lay some moss green over the back and felt it in

Lay some green over the end of the tail feather and felt it in

Actual size - components

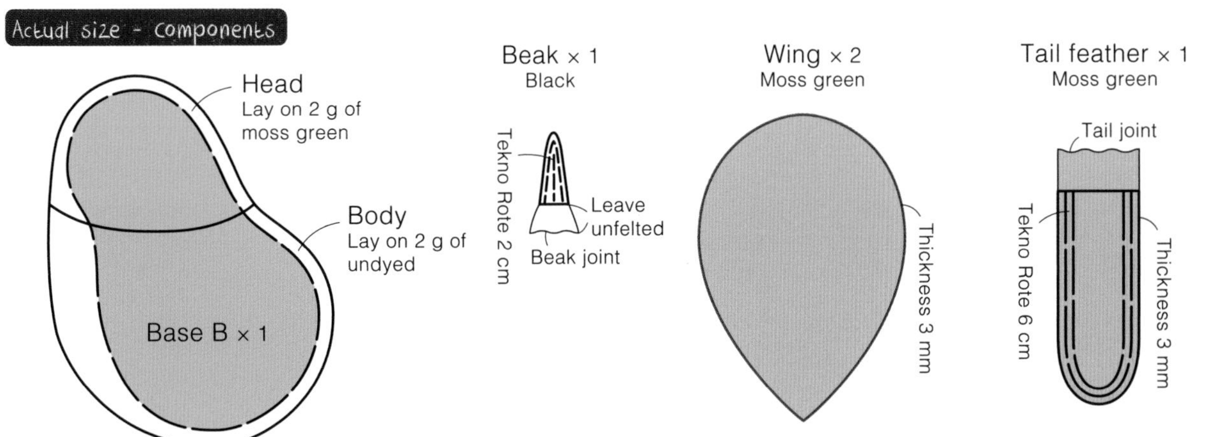
Head
Lay on 2 g of moss green
Body
Lay on 2 g of undyed
Base B × 1
Beak × 1
Black
Tekno Rote 2 cm
Leave unfelted
Beak joint
Wing × 2
Moss green
Thickness 3 mm
Tail feather × 1
Moss green
Tail joint
Tekno Rote 6 cm
Thickness 3 mm

24 Tree sparrow

Materials

Felt wool

- Solid
  - •Off-white, 3 g
  - •Chestnut, 2 g
  - •Brown
  - •Dark brown, small amounts
- Natural Blend
  - •Light beige, 2 g
  - •Undyed, small amount
- Mix
  - •Brown, 2 g

Solid eyes •3 mm x 2

Other materials

- •Clear plastic wallet 2 cm × 11 cm
- •Floral wire (brown, 24 gauge) 8 x 3-cm lengths
- •Tekno Rote 8 cm
- •Floral tape, amount to suit

Instructions

※For basic instructions to help you make the birds, see pp.34 to 40. For the beak, see p.66.

1 Make the base.

2 Felt the wool of the head and body to the base.

3 Lay the wool indicated in the instructions over the head and body and felt it on.

4 Make and attach the tail feather.

5 Make and attach the wings.

6 Make and attach the beak.

7 Make the face.

8 Make and attach the legs.

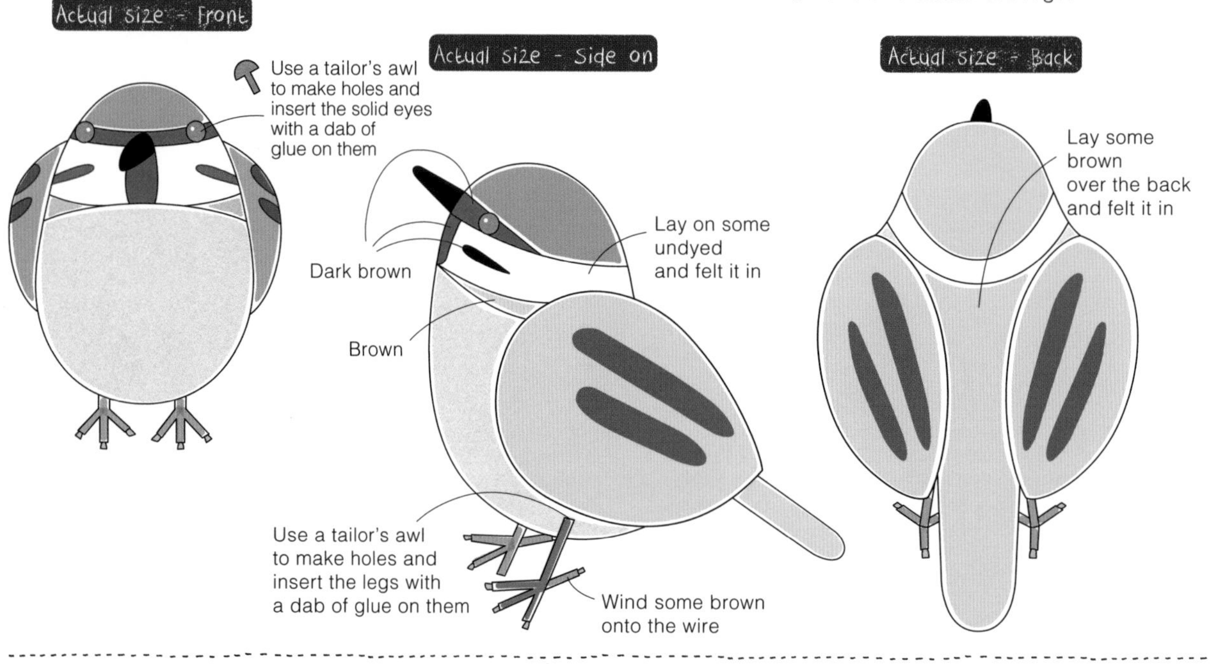
Actual size - Front
Use a tailor's awl to make holes and insert the solid eyes with a dab of glue on them
Actual size - Side on
Dark brown
Lay on some undyed and felt it in
Brown
Use a tailor's awl to make holes and insert the legs with a dab of glue on them
Wind some brown onto the wire
Actual size - Back
Lay some brown over the back and felt it in

Actual size - components

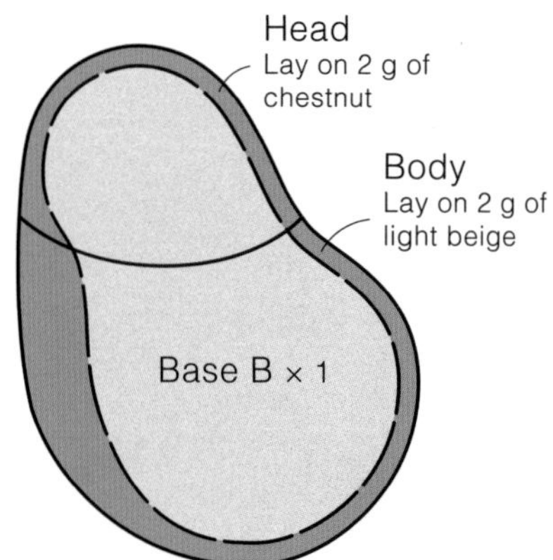
Head
Lay on 2 g of chestnut
Body
Lay on 2 g of light beige
Base B × 1

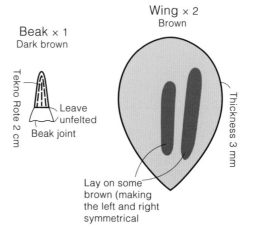

Beak × 1
Dark brown

Tekno Rote 2 cm
Leave unfelted
Beak joint

Wing × 2
Brown

Thickness 3 mm
Lay on some brown (making the left and right symmetrical

Tail feather × 1
Brown

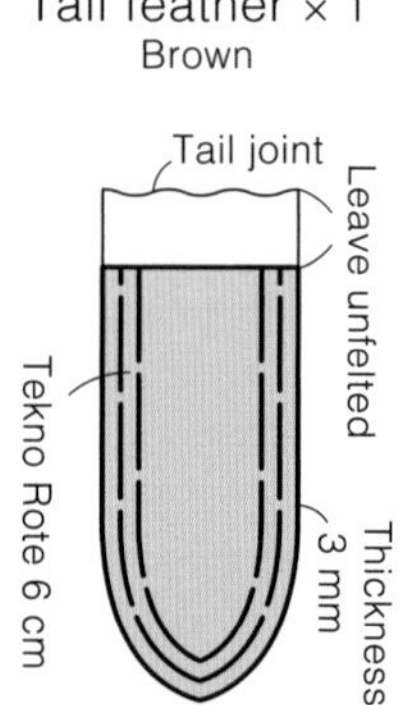
Tail joint
Leave unfelted
Tekno Rote 6 cm
Thickness 3 mm

25 Kingfisher

Materials

Felt wool

Solid	•Off-white, 3 g •Indigo, 2 g •Orange, 1.5 g •Sky blue, 1 g •White, small amount
Mix	•Mustard, 1.5 g •Black •Navy blue, small amounts

Solid eyes •3 mm x 2

Other materials

- •Clear plastic wallet 2 cm × 11 cm
- •Floral wire (brown, 24 gauge) 8 x 3-cm lengths
- •Tekno Rote 12 cm
- •Floral tape, amount to suit

Instructions

※For basic instructions to help you make the birds, see pp.34 to 40. For the beak, see p.66.

1 Make the base.

2 Felt the wool of the head and body onto the base.

3 Lay the wool indicated in the instructions over the head and felt it on.

4 Make and attach the tail feather.

5 Make and attach the wings.

6 Make and attach the beak.

7 Make the face.

8 Make and attach the legs.

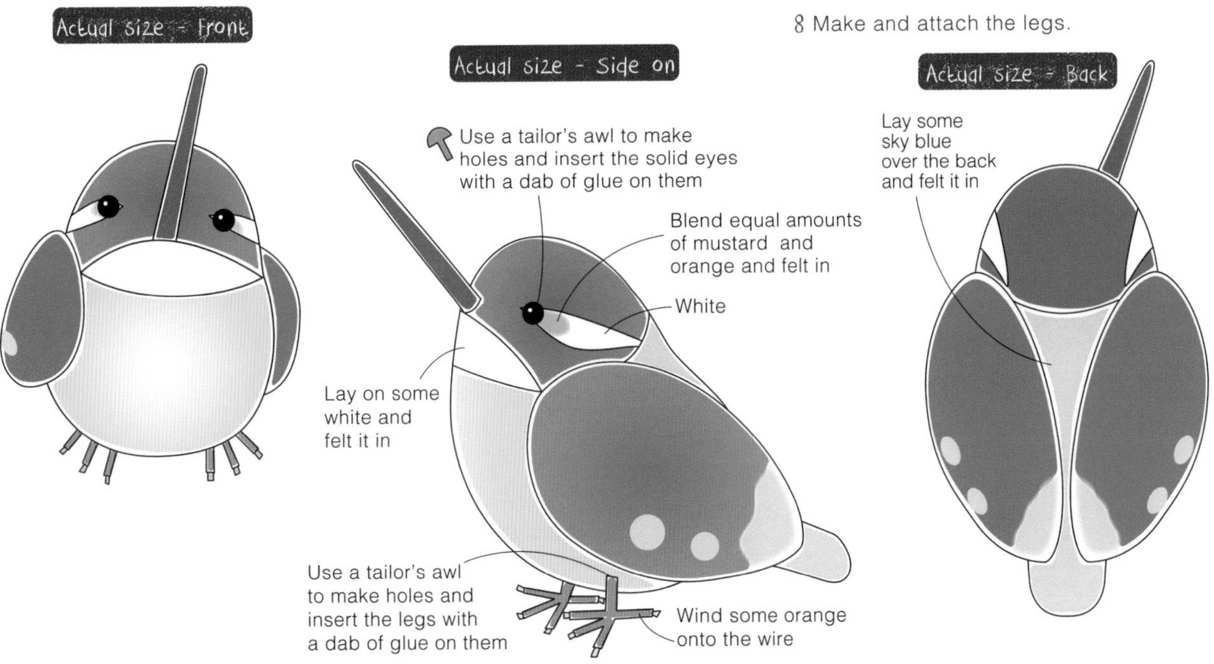
Actual size - Front
Actual size - Side on
Use a tailor's awl to make holes and insert the solid eyes with a dab of glue on them
Blend equal amounts of mustard and orange and felt in
White
Lay on some white and felt it in
Use a tailor's awl to make holes and insert the legs with a dab of glue on them
Wind some orange onto the wire
Actual size - Back
Lay some sky blue over the back and felt it in

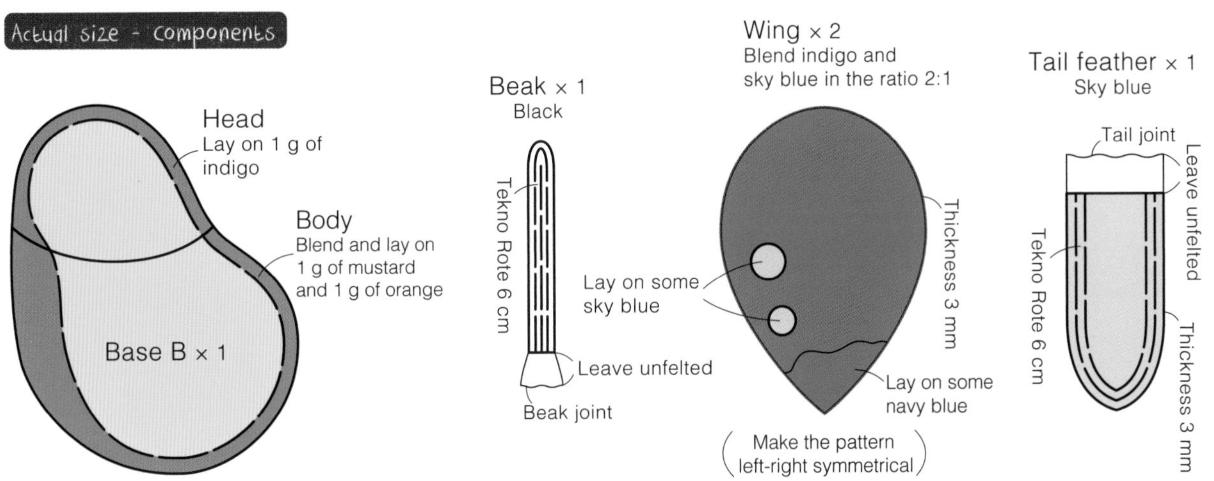
Actual size - components
Head
Lay on 1 g of indigo
Body
Blend and lay on 1 g of mustard and 1 g of orange
Base B × 1
Beak × 1
Black
Tekno Rote 6 cm
Leave unfelted
Beak joint
Wing × 2
Blend indigo and sky blue in the ratio 2:1
Thickness 3 mm
Lay on some sky blue
Lay on some navy blue
Make the pattern left-right symmetrical
Tail feather × 1
Sky blue
Tail joint
Leave unfelted
Tekno Rote 6 cm
Thickness 3 mm

Page 25

26 Cuban tody

Materials

Felt wool

Solid
- •Off-white, 3 g
- •Moss green, 3 g
- •Violet blue
- •Dark yellow-green
- •Sky blue, small amounts

Natural Blend
- •Undyed, 2 g
- •Pink •Red
- •Green, small amounts

Mix
- •Mustard, small amount

Solid eyes •3 mm x 2

Other materials

- •Clear plastic wallet 2 cm x 11 cm
- •Floral wire (brown, 24 gauge) 8 x 3-cm lengths
- •Tekno Rote 16 cm
- •Floral tape, amount to suit

Instructions

※For basic instructions to help you make the birds, see pp.34 to 40. For the beak, see p.66.

1 Make the base.

2 Felt the wool of the head and body onto the base.

3 Lay the wool indicated in the instructions over the head and body and then felt it on.

4 Make and attach the tail feather.

5 Make and attach the wings.

6 Make and attach the beak.

7 Make the face.

8 Make and attach the legs.

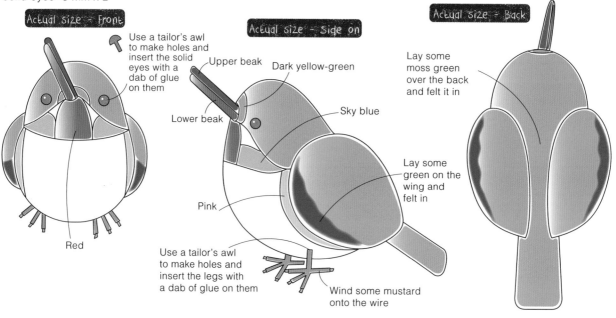

Actual size - Front

Use a tailor's awl to make holes and insert the solid eyes with a dab of glue on them

Red

Actual size - Side on

Upper beak

Dark yellow-green

Lower beak

Sky blue

Pink

Use a tailor's awl to make holes and insert the legs with a dab of glue on them

Wind some mustard onto the wire

Lay some green on the wing and felt in

Actual size - Back

Lay some moss green over the back and felt it in

Actual size - components

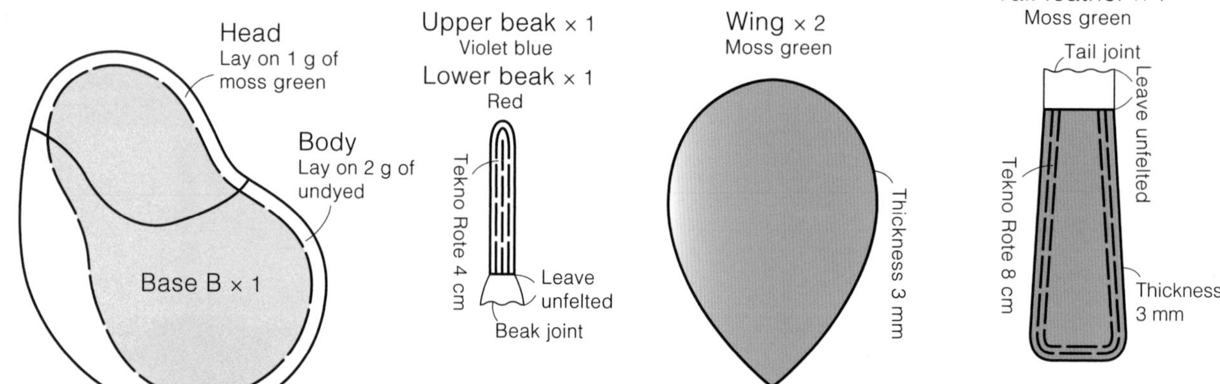
Head
Lay on 1 g of moss green
Body
Lay on 2 g of undyed
Base B × 1
Upper beak × 1
Violet blue
Lower beak × 1
Red
Tekno Rote 4 cm
Leave unfelted
Beak joint
Wing × 2
Moss green
Thickness 3 mm
Tail feather × 1
Moss green
Tail joint
Leave unfelted
Tekno Rote 8 cm
Thickness 3 mm

Page 25

27 Lilac-breasted roller

Materials

Felt wool

Solid	•Off-white, 3 g •Salmon pink •Sky blue, small amounts
Natural Blend	•Brown, 4 g •Mint, 1 g •Pink, small amount
Mix	•Black •Undyed, small amounts

Hamanaka solid eyes •3 mm x 2

Other materials

•Clear plastic wallet 2 cm × 11 cm
•Floral wire (brown, 24 gauge) 8 x 3-cm lengths
•Tekno Rote 11 cm
•Floral tape, amount to suit

Instructions

※For basic instructions to help you make the birds, see pp.34 to 40. For the beak, see p.66.

1 Make the base.

2 Felt the wool of the head and body onto the base.

3 Lay the wool indicated in the instructions over the head and body and felt it on.

4 Make and attach the tail feather.

5 Make and attach the wings.

6 Make and attach the beak.

7 Make the face.

8 Make and attach the legs.

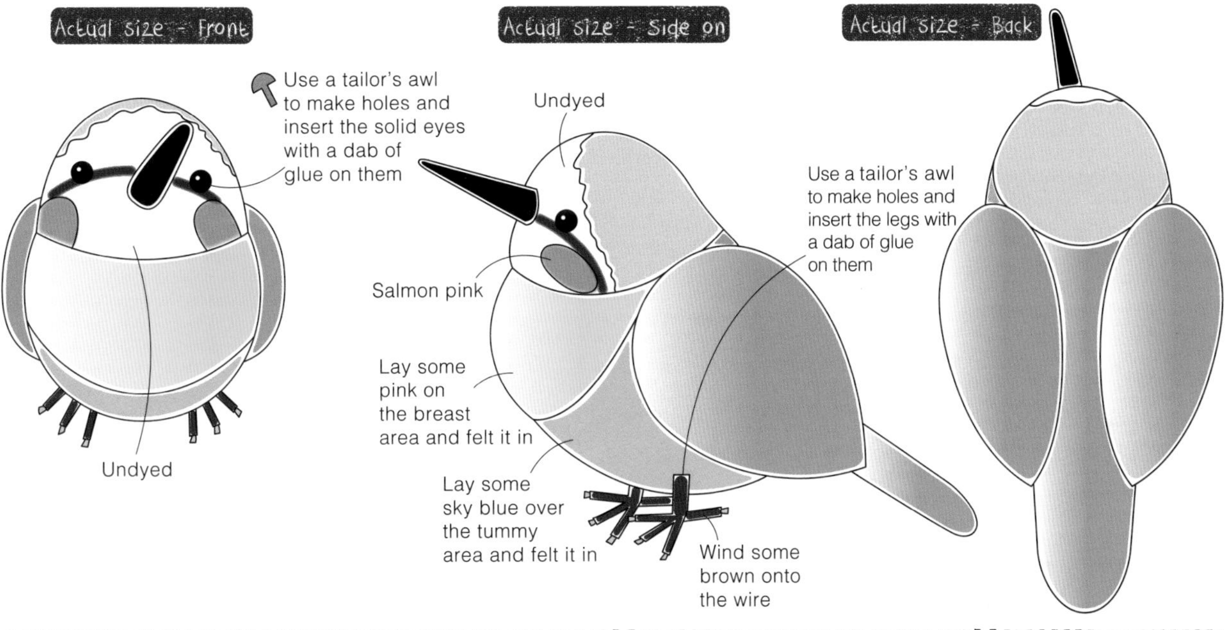
Actual size - Front
Actual size - Side on
Actual size - Back
Use a tailor's awl to make holes and insert the solid eyes with a dab of glue on them
Undyed
Undyed
Salmon pink
Lay some pink on the breast area and felt it in
Lay some sky blue over the tummy area and felt it in
Wind some brown onto the wire
Use a tailor's awl to make holes and insert the legs with a dab of glue on them

Actual size - components

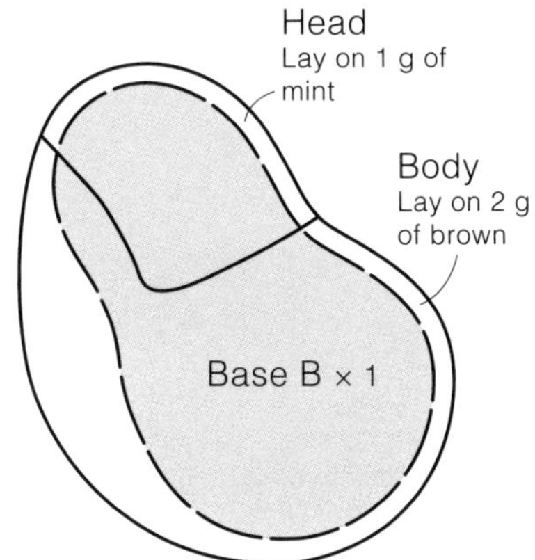
Head
Lay on 1 g of mint
Body
Lay on 2 g of brown
Base B × 1

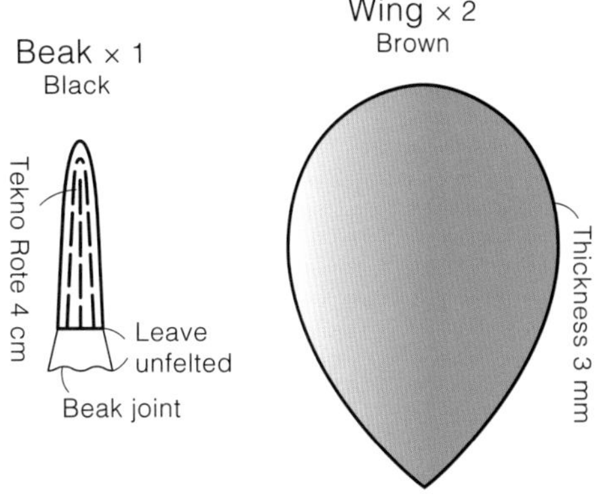
Beak × 1
Black
Tekno Rote 4 cm
Leave unfelted
Beak joint
Wing × 2
Brown
Thickness 3 mm

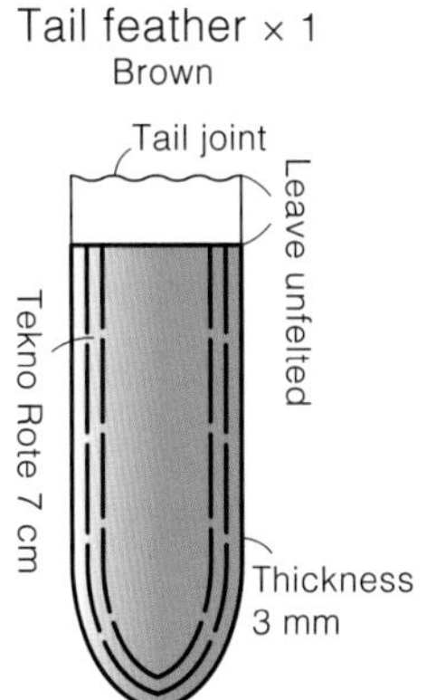
Tail feather × 1
Brown
Tail joint
Leave unfelted
Tekno Rote 7 cm
Thickness 3 mm

Page 26 28 Flamingo

Materials

Felt wool

Solid
- •Off-white, 7 g
- •Madder red •Black
- •Bitter orange, small amounts

Natural Blend
- •Light pink, 6 g

Solid eyes •2 mm x 2

Other materials
- •Clear plastic wallet 2 cm × 13 cm
- •Floral wire (brown, 24 gauge) 8 x 10-cm lengths
- •Tekno Rote 24 cm
- •Floral tape, amount to suit

Instructions

※For basic instructions to help you make the birds, see pp.34 to 40.

1 Make the base for the body with Needle Watawata, using the actual-size components to help you.

2 Felt the wool of the body onto the base.

3 Felt the wool onto the Tekno Rote, attach it to the body, and then make the neck, head, and beak.

4 Make and attach the wings.

5 Make the face.

6 Make and attach the legs.

How to make the neck head, and beak

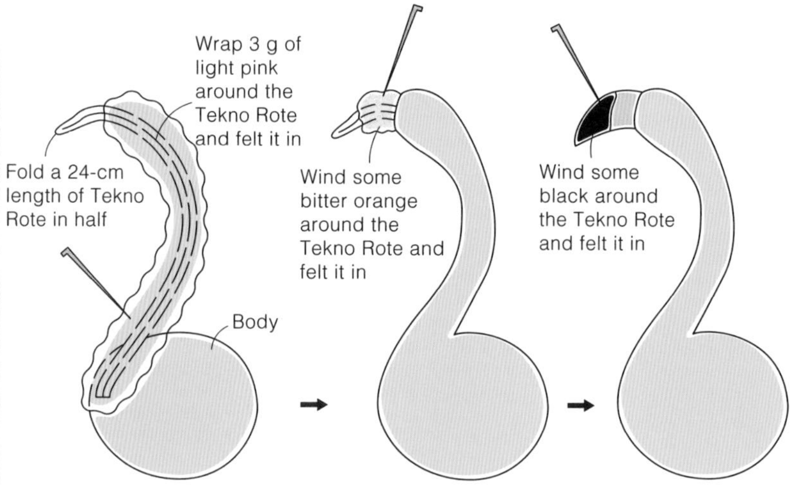

Fold a 24-cm length of Tekno Rote in half
Wrap 3 g of light pink around the Tekno Rote and felt it in
Body
Wind some bitter orange around the Tekno Rote and felt it in
Wind some black around the Tekno Rote and felt it in

Actual size components

Wing × 2
Light pink
Thickness 3 mm
Body
Lay on 2 g of light pink
Body base × 1
Needle Watawata
Off-white
Make into an oval shape

How to make the legs

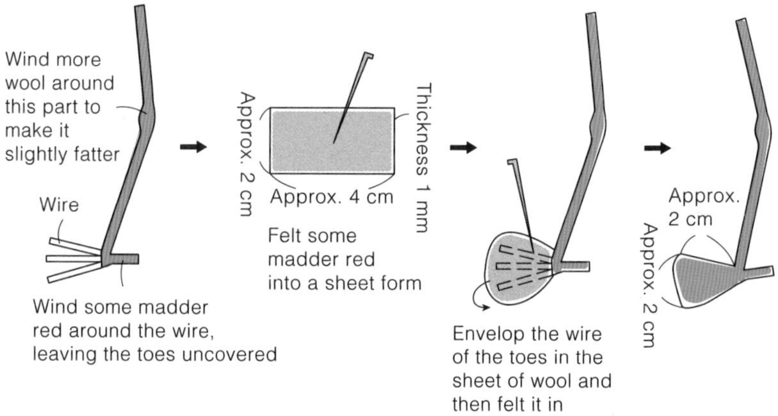

Wind more wool around this part to make it slightly fatter
Wire
Wind some madder red around the wire, leaving the toes uncovered
Approx. 2 cm
Approx. 4 cm
Thickness 1 mm
Felt some madder red into a sheet form
Envelop the wire of the toes in the sheet of wool and then felt it in
Approx. 2 cm
Approx. 2 cm

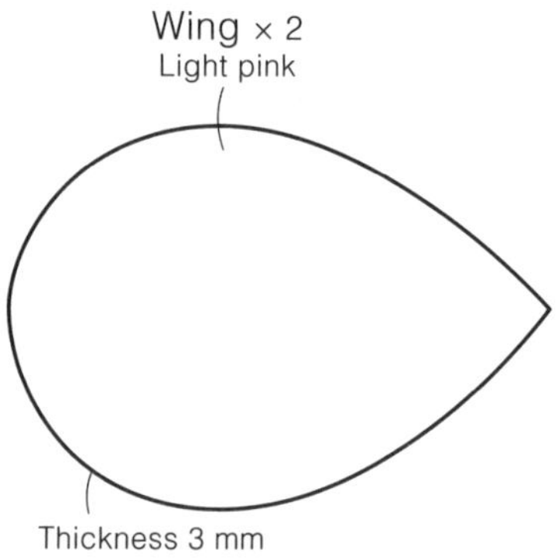

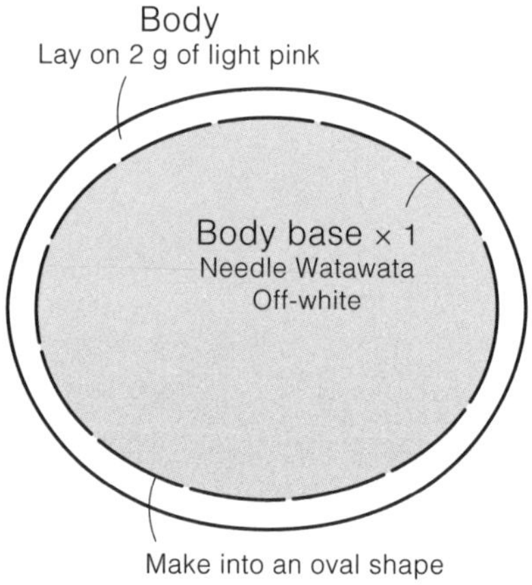

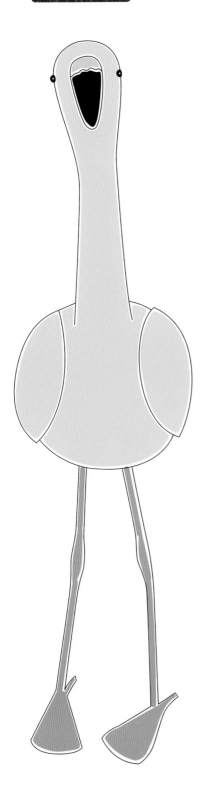

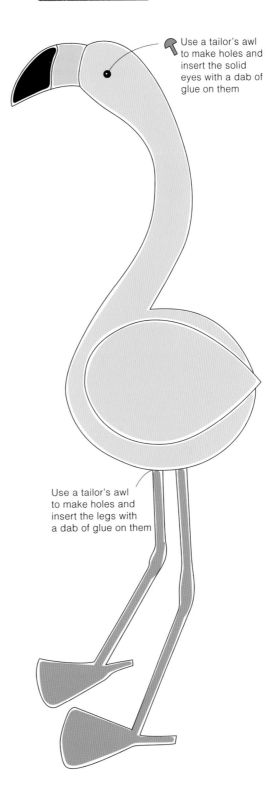

Actual size – Front

Actual size – Side on

Use a tailor's awl to make holes and insert the solid eyes with a dab of glue on them

Use a tailor's awl to make holes and insert the legs with a dab of glue on them

29 Shoebill

Materials

Felt wool

Needle Watawata
•Off-white, 6 g
Solid •Young leaf, small amount
Natural Blend
•Grey 8 g
Mix •Mustard, 2 g

Solid eyes •3 mm x 2

Other materials

•Clear plastic wallet 2 cm × 16 cm
•Floral wire (brown, 24 gauge)
8 x 10-cm lengths
•Floral tape, amount to suit

Instructions

※For basic instructions to help you make the birds, see pp.34 to 40.

1 Make the bases for the head and body with Needle Watawata, using the actual-size components to help you.
2 Felt the wool for the head and body onto their respective bases.
3 Make the neck and join the head and body together.
4 Make and attach the tail feather.
5 Make and attach the wings.
6 Make and attach the beak.
7 Make the face.
8 Make and attach the legs.

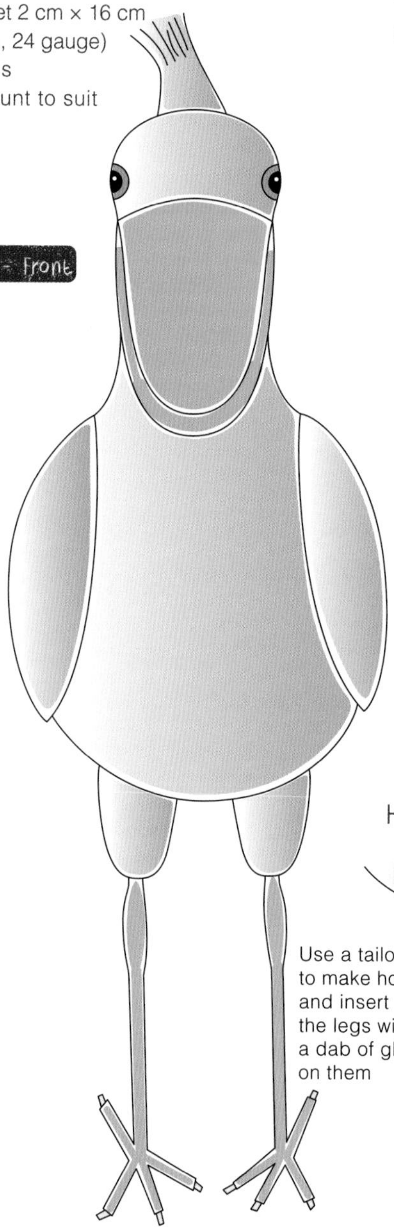

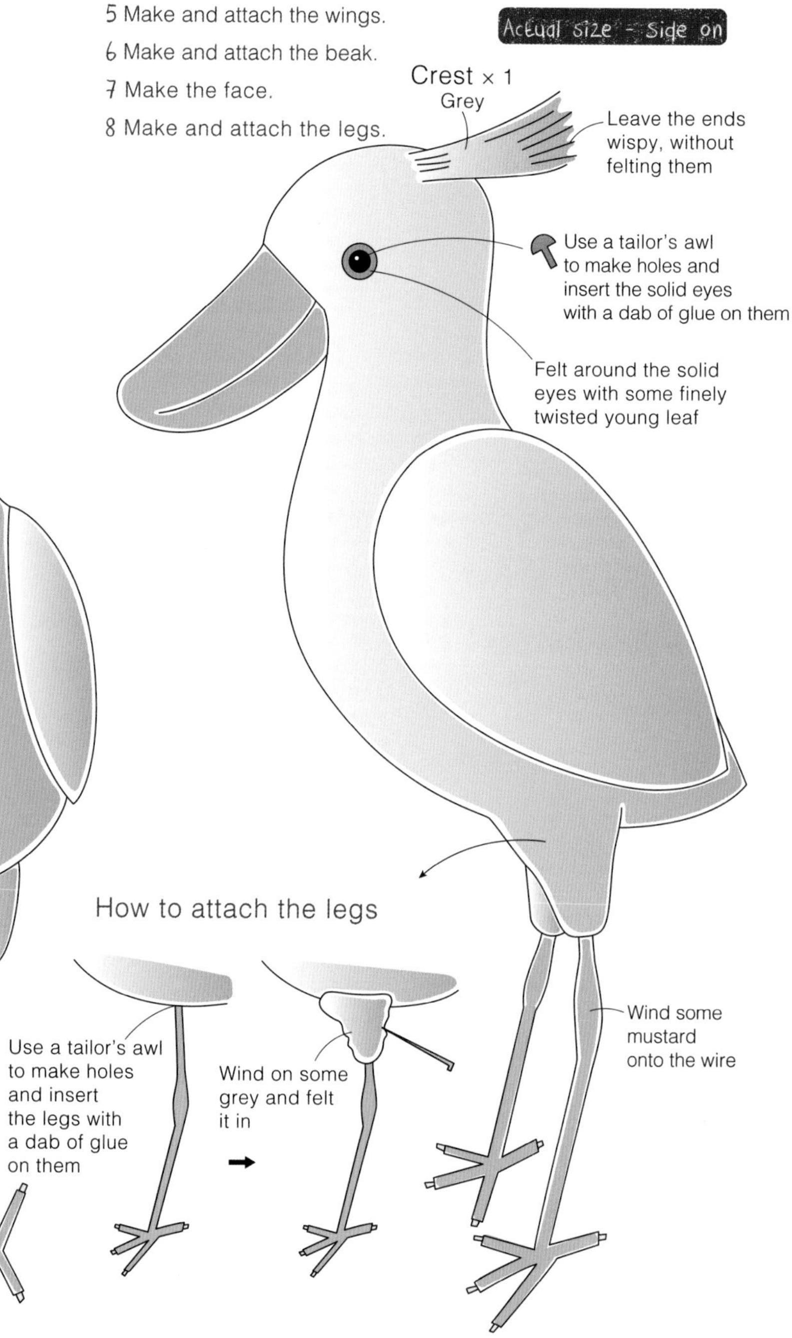

Actual size - Front
Actual size - Side on
Crest × 1
Grey
Leave the ends wispy, without felting them
Use a tailor's awl to make holes and insert the solid eyes with a dab of glue on them
Felt around the solid eyes with some finely twisted young leaf
How to attach the legs
Use a tailor's awl to make holes and insert the legs with a dab of glue on them
Wind on some grey and felt it in
Wind some mustard onto the wire

Actual size – Back

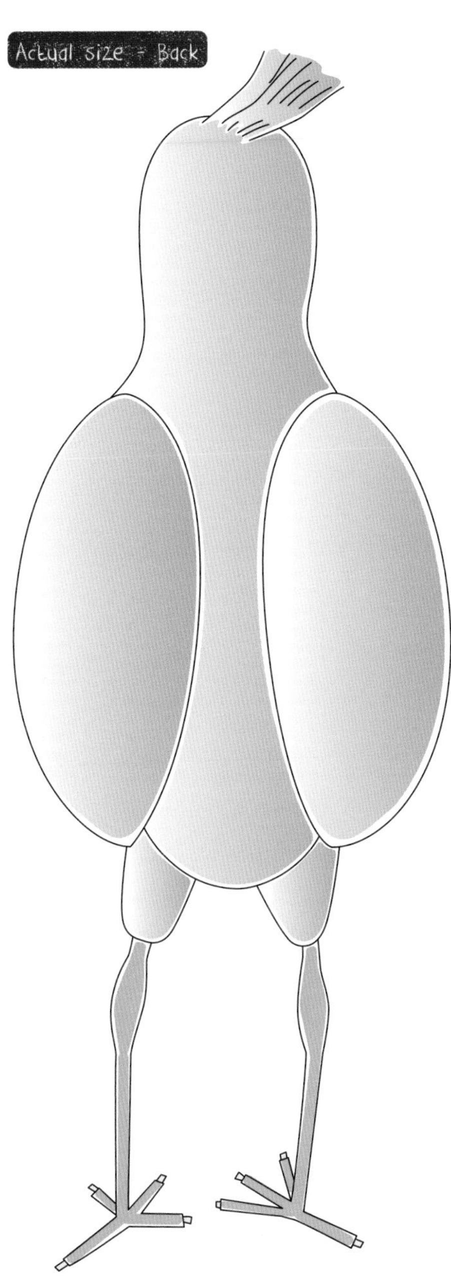

How to join the head, neck, and body

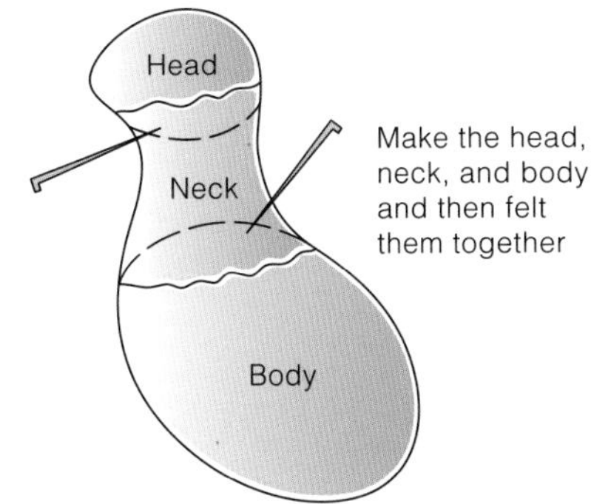
Head
Neck
Body
Make the head, neck, and body and then felt them together

Actual size – components

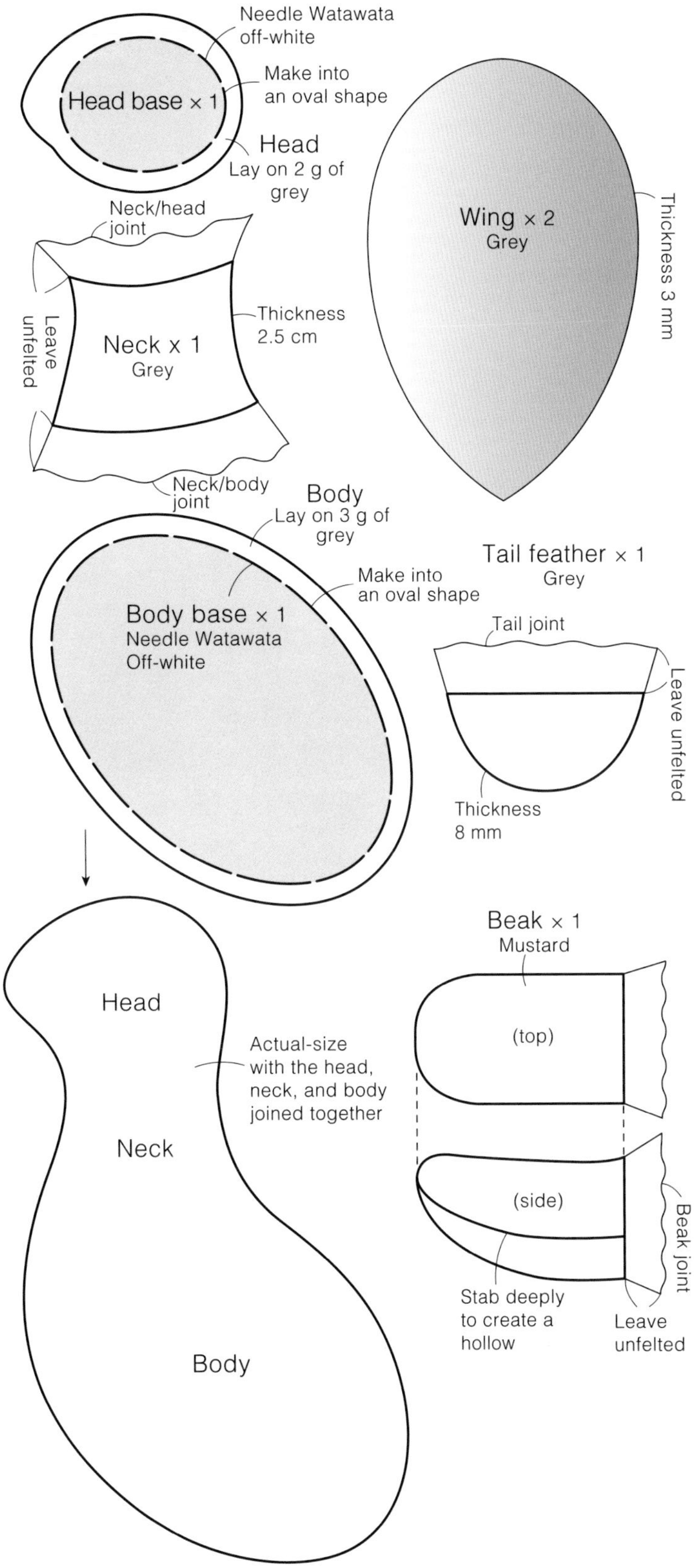

Head base × 1
Needle Watawata off-white
Make into an oval shape
Head
Lay on 2 g of grey

Neck × 1
Grey
Neck/head joint
Leave unfelted
Thickness 2.5 cm
Neck/body joint

Wing × 2
Grey
Thickness 3 mm

Body base × 1
Needle Watawata Off-white
Body
Lay on 3 g of grey
Make into an oval shape

Tail feather × 1
Grey
Tail joint
Leave unfelted
Thickness 8 mm

Head
Neck
Body
Actual-size with the head, neck, and body joined together

Beak × 1
Mustard
(top)
(side)
Beak joint
Stab deeply to create a hollow
Leave unfelted

Page 28

30 Brooch (scarlet macaw)

Materials

Felt wool

- Solid •Indigo, small amount
- Natural Blend
  - •Red, 2 g
  - •Undyed •Light beige
  - •Pale orange, small amounts

Solid eye •2 mm x 1

Other materials

- •Felt 5 cm x 5 cm
- •Brooch pin (20 mm) x 1

Instructions

※For basic instructions to help you make the brooch, see pp.42 and 43.

1 Make the body.

2 Make and attach the tail feather.

3 Make and attach the wings.

4 Make and attach the beak.

5 Make the face.

6 Make the backing patch and slide the brooch pin through it.

7 Glue the backing patch onto the reverse.

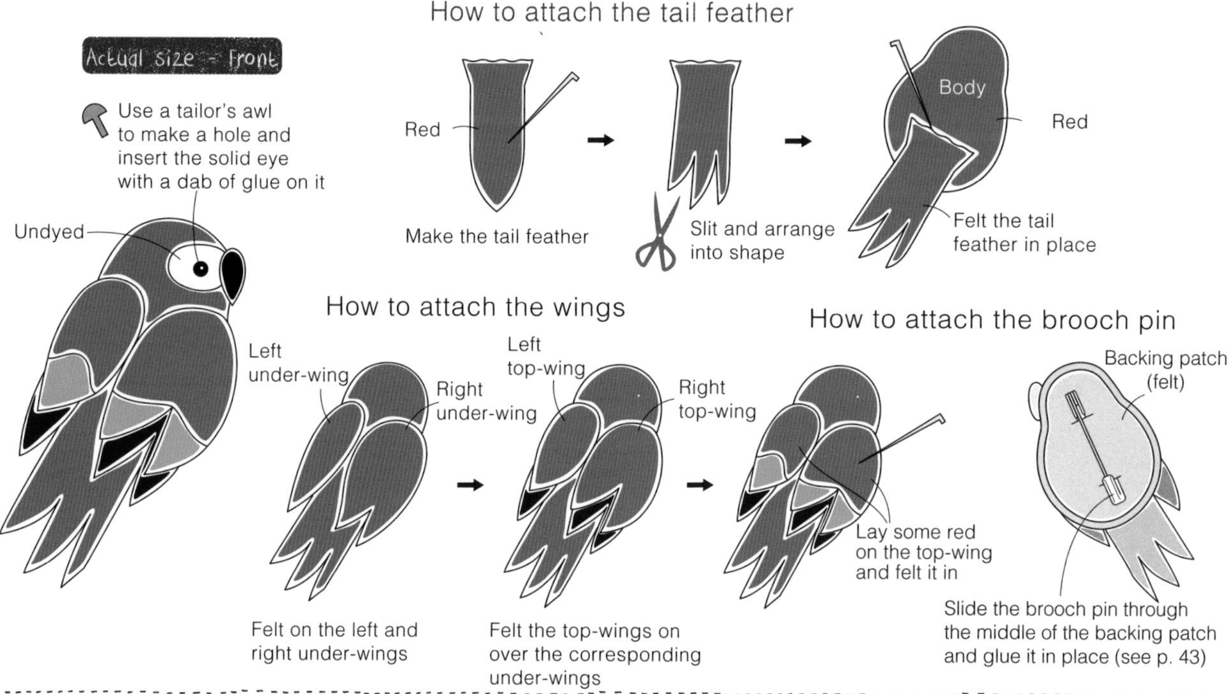

How to attach the tail feather
Actual size - front
Use a tailor's awl to make a hole and insert the solid eye with a dab of glue on it
Undyed
Red
Make the tail feather
Slit and arrange into shape
Body
Red
Felt the tail feather in place
How to attach the wings
Left under-wing
Right under-wing
Left top-wing
Right top-wing
Felt on the left and right under-wings
Felt the top-wings on over the corresponding under-wings
How to attach the brooch pin
Lay some red on the top-wing and felt it in
Backing patch (felt)
Slide the brooch pin through the middle of the backing patch and glue it in place (see p. 43)

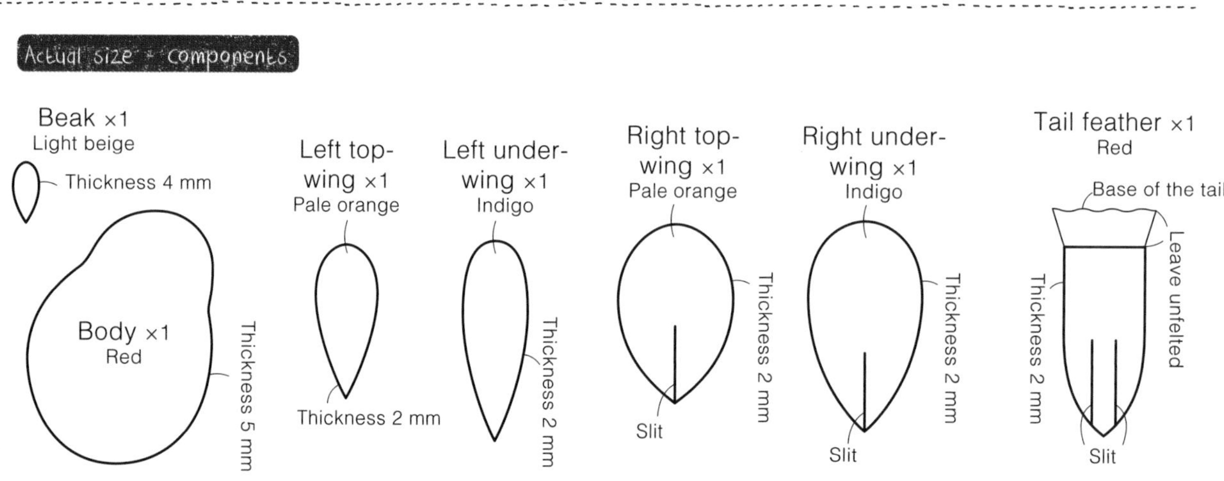

Actual size - components
Beak ×1
Light beige
Thickness 4 mm
Body ×1
Red
Thickness 5 mm
Left top-wing ×1
Pale orange
Thickness 2 mm
Left under-wing ×1
Indigo
Thickness 2 mm
Right top-wing ×1
Pale orange
Thickness 2 mm
Slit
Right under-wing ×1
Indigo
Thickness 2 mm
Slit
Tail feather ×1
Red
Base of the tail
Leave unfelted
Thickness 2 mm
Slit

Page 28

31 Brooch (budgerigar)

Materials

Felt wool

Solid •Yellow-green, 2 g •Violet-blue, small amount
Natural Blend
•Light beige •Custard, small amounts
Mix •Black, small amount

Solid eye •2 mm x 1

Other materials

•Felt 5 cm x 5 cm
•Brooch pin (20 mm) x 1

Instructions

※ For basic instructions to help you make the brooch, see pp.42 and 43.

1 Make the head and body and felt them together.
2 Make and attach the tail feather.
3 Make and attach the wings.
4 Make and attach the beak.
5 Make the face.
6 Make the backing patch and slide the brooch pin through it.
7 Glue the backing patch onto the reverse.

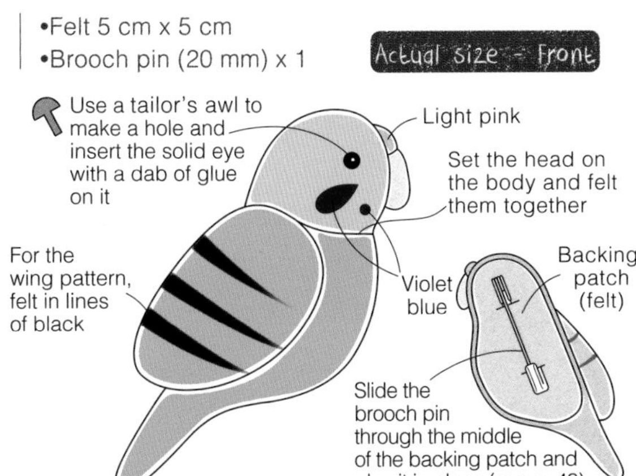
Actual size - Front
Use a tailor's awl to make a hole and insert the solid eye with a dab of glue on it
Light pink
Set the head on the body and felt them together
For the wing pattern, felt in lines of black
Violet blue
Backing patch (felt)
Slide the brooch pin through the middle of the backing patch and glue it in place (see p. 43)

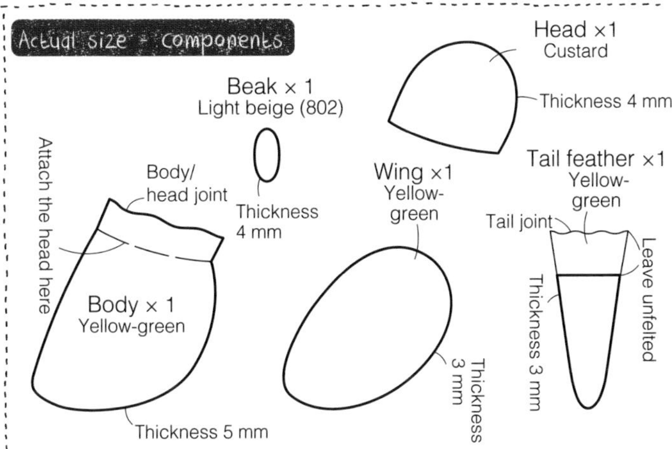
Actual size - Components
Head ×1
Custard
Thickness 4 mm
Beak × 1
Light beige (802)
Attach the head here
Body/ head joint
Thickness 4 mm
Wing ×1
Yellow-green
Tail feather ×1
Yellow-green
Tail joint
Leave unfelted
Thickness 3 mm
Body × 1
Yellow-green
Thickness 3 mm
Thickness 5 mm

Page 28

32 Brooch (owl)

Materials

Felt wool

Solid •Golden yellow, small amount
Natural Blend
•Light beige, 1 g •Undyed, small amount
Mix •Brown, small amount

Solid eyes •3 mm x 2

Other materials

•Felt 5 cm x 5 cm
•Brooch pin (20 mm) x 1

Instructions

※For basic instructions to help you make the brooch, see pp.42 and 43.

1 Make the body.
2 Attach the face.
3 Make and attach the beak.
4 Attach the eyes.
5 Make the backing patch and slide the brooch pin through it.
6 Glue the backing patch onto the reverse.

※The actual-size components are on p.78

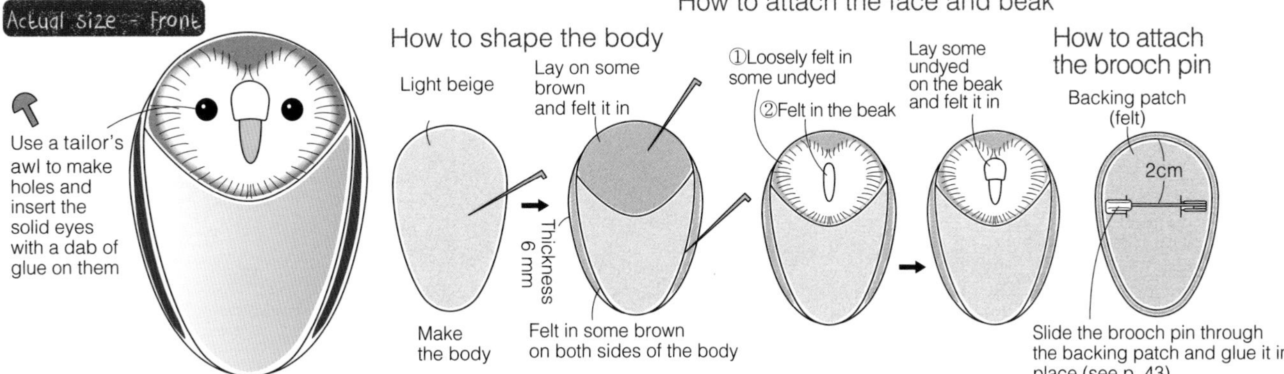
Actual size - Front
Use a tailor's awl to make holes and insert the solid eyes with a dab of glue on them
How to attach the face and beak
How to shape the body
Light beige
Lay on some brown and felt it in
Thickness 6 mm
Make the body
Felt in some brown on both sides of the body
①Loosely felt in some undyed
②Felt in the beak
Lay some undyed on the beak and felt it in
How to attach the brooch pin
Backing patch (felt)
2cm
Slide the brooch pin through the backing patch and glue it in place (see p. 43)

Page 28

34 Brooch (Major Mitchell's cockatoo)

Materials

Felt wool

Solid •Pale pink, 1 g •Light pink, small amount
Natural Blend
•Undyed •Light beige
•Red, small amounts

Solid eye •2 mm x 1

Other materials

•Felt 5 cm × 5 cm
•Brooch pin (20 mm) x 1

Instructions

※For basic instructions to help you make the brooch, see pp.42 and 43.

1 Make the body.
2 Make and attach the crest.
3 Make and attach the beak.
4 Attach the eyes.
5 Make the backing patch and slide the brooch pin through it.
6 Glue the backing patch onto the reverse.

32 Actual size - Front

Use a tailor's awl to make holes and insert the solid eyes with a dab of glue on them

How to shape the body

Pale pink

Make the base for the body

Lay on some light pink and felt it in

Lay on some undyed and felt it in

How to attach the crest

Light pink

Make the base for the crest

Lay over some red and felt it in

Make slits and arrange into shape

Reverse of the crest

Reverse of the body

Felt on the crest, working from the reverse side of the body

How to shape the body

Felt in some red

Felt the beak in place

How to attach brooch pin

Backing patch (felt)

Pass the brooch pin through the middle of the backing patch and glue it in place (see p.43)

32 Actual size - components

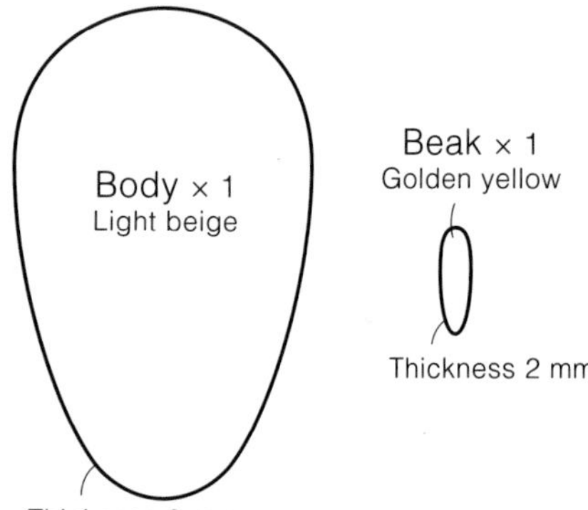
Body × 1
Light beige
Thickness 6 mm
Beak × 1
Golden yellow
Thickness 2 mm

34 Actual size - components

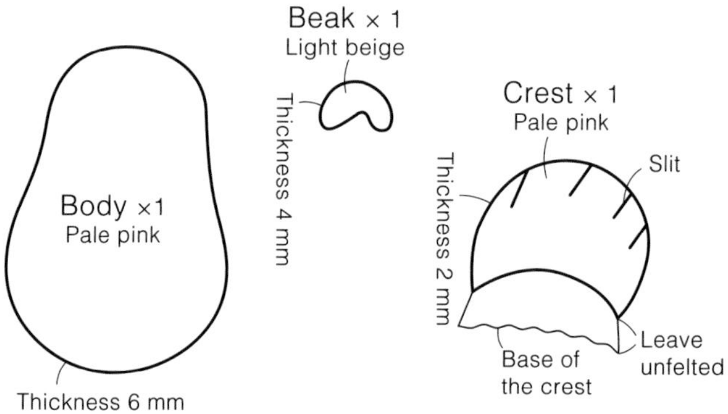
Body ×1
Pale pink
Thickness 6 mm
Beak × 1
Light beige
Thickness 4 mm
Crest × 1
Pale pink
Slit
Thickness 2 mm
Base of the crest
Leave unfelted

Page 29

35 Eggs

Materials

Felt wool

Solid
- •Off-white, 20 g
- •Saxe blue •Light pink, 4 g of each
- •White •Yellow-green •Young leaf
- •Orange, small amounts

Natural Blend
- •Custard •Sherbet orange
- •Mint, 4 g of each

Instructions

1 Make five egg bases with Needle Watawata, using the actual-size components to help you.

2 Felt the different coloured wools onto their bases.

3 Felt the wool into the alphabet shapes.

4 Felt the wool into the shapes of the flower core, petals, and leaves.

※All of the alphabet letters are in white

※Roll the wool into balls for the flower cores, and into long, thin shapes for the petals and leaves, and then felt them in.

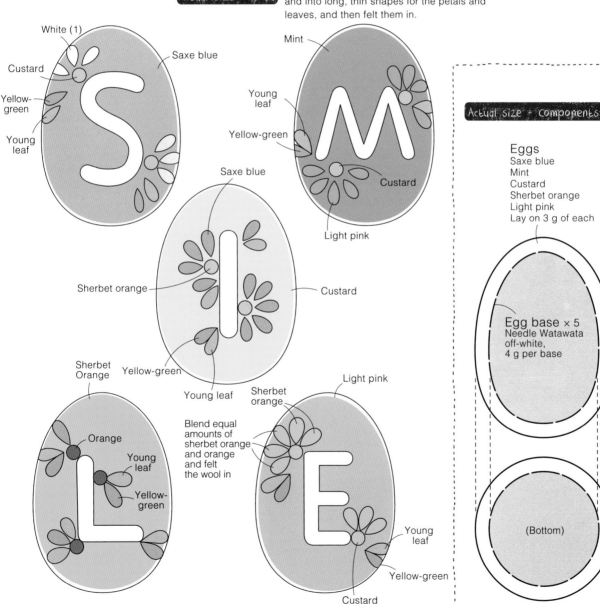

Actual size - front

White (1)
Saxe blue
Custard
Yellow-green
Young leaf

Mint
Young leaf
Yellow-green
Custard
Light pink

Saxe blue
Sherbet orange
Custard
Yellow-green
Young leaf

Sherbet Orange
Orange
Young leaf
Yellow-green

Light pink
Sherbet orange
Blend equal amounts of sherbet orange and orange and felt the wool in
Young leaf
Yellow-green
Custard

Actual size - components

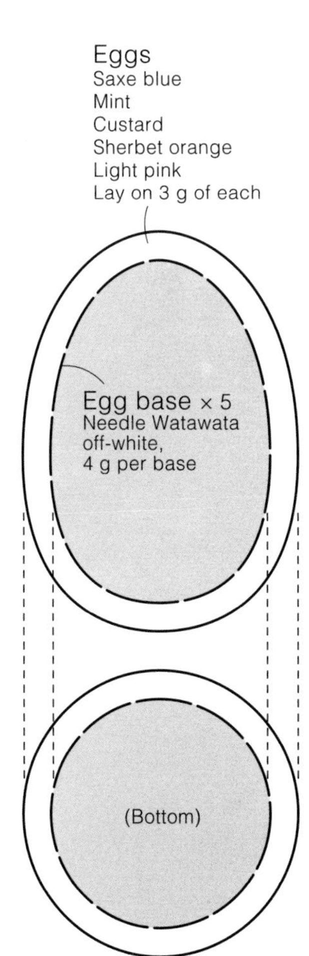
Eggs
Saxe blue
Mint
Custard
Sherbet orange
Light pink
Lay on 3 g of each
Egg base × 5
Needle Watawata
off-white,
4 g per base
(Bottom)

12 Actual size - components

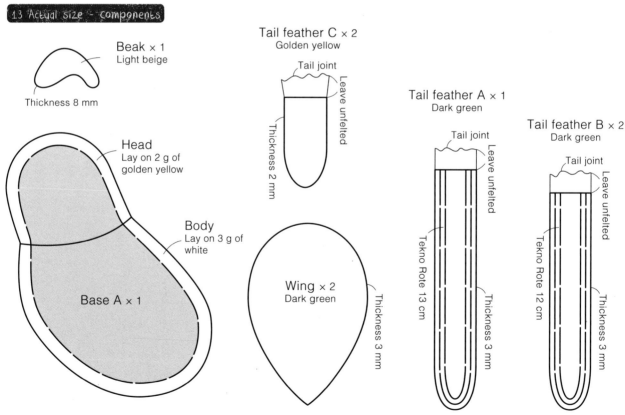

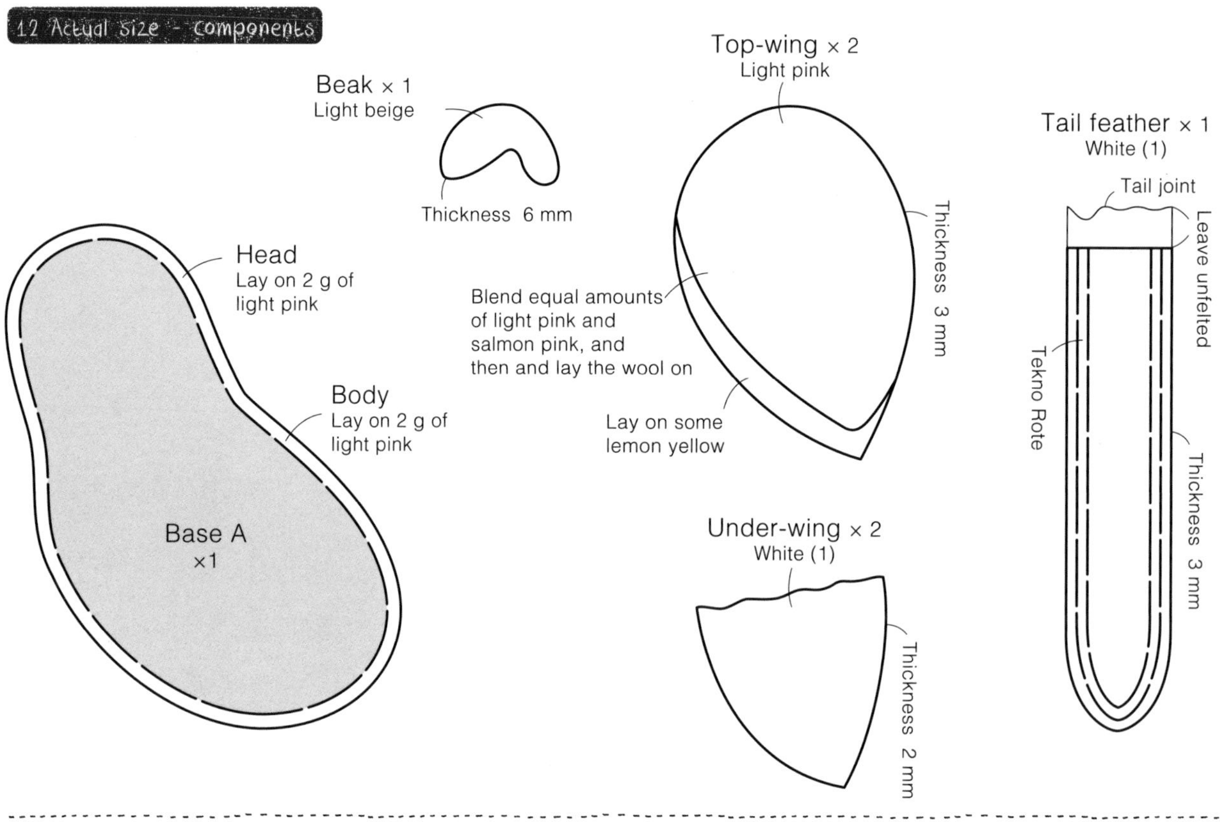
Beak × 1
Light beige
Thickness 6 mm
Top-wing × 2
Light pink
Thickness 3 mm
Blend equal amounts of light pink and salmon pink, and then and lay the wool on
Lay on some lemon yellow
Tail feather × 1
White (1)
Tail joint
Leave unfelted
Tekno Rote
Thickness 3 mm
Head
Lay on 2 g of light pink
Body
Lay on 2 g of light pink
Base A
×1
Under-wing × 2
White (1)
Thickness 2 mm

13 Actual size - components

Beak × 1
Light beige

Thickness 8 mm

Tail feather C × 2
Golden yellow

Tail joint

Leave unfelted

Thickness 2 mm

Tail feather A × 1
Dark green

Tail joint

Leave unfelted

Tekno Rote 13 cm

Thickness 3 mm

Tail feather B × 2
Dark green

Tail joint

Leave unfelted

Tekno Rote 12 cm

Thickness 3 mm

Head
Lay on 2 g of golden yellow

Body
Lay on 3 g of white

Base A × 1

Wing × 2
Dark green

Thickness 3 mm